Contents

Introduction 1

Foundational Risk Management 5
    Risk Identification 5

Internal Controls 7
    Scope of Internal Controls 7
    Internal Audit 7
    Independent Model Review and Validation 7
    Policies and Procedures 8
    Ensuring Integrity of Results 8
    Documentation 9

Governance 11
    Board of Directors 11
    Board Reporting 11
    Senior Management 12
    Documenting Decisions 12

Capital Policy 13
    Capital Goals and Targets 14
    Capital Contingency Plan 14

BHC Scenario Design 17
    Scenario Design and Severity 17
    Variable Coverage 18
    Clear Narratives 18

Estimation Methodologies for Losses, Revenues, and Expenses 19
    General Expectations 19
    Loss-Estimation Methodologies 22
    PPNR Projection Methodologies 31

Assessing Capital Adequacy Impact 37
    Balance Sheet and RWAs 37
    Allowance for Loan and Lease Losses (ALLL) 38
    Aggregation of Projections 38

Concluding Observations 41

Introduction

The Federal Reserve has previously noted the importance of capital planning at large, complex bank holding companies (BHCs). Capital is central to a BHC's ability to absorb unexpected losses and continue to lend to creditworthy businesses and consumers. It serves as the first line of defense against losses, protecting the deposit insurance fund and taxpayers. As such, a large BHC's processes for managing and allocating its capital resources are critical not only to its individual health and performance, but also to the stability and effective functioning of the U.S. financial system. The Federal Reserve's Capital Plan Rule and the associated annual Comprehensive Capital Analysis and Review (CCAR) have emphasized the importance the Federal Reserve places on BHCs' internal capital planning processes, and on the supervisory assessment of all aspects of these processes, which is a key element of a supervisory program that is focused on promoting resiliency at the largest BHCs.[1]

These initiatives have focused not just on the amount of capital that a BHC has, but also on the internal practices and policies a firm uses to determine the amount and composition of capital that would be adequate, given the firm's risk exposures and corporate strategies as well as supervisory expectations and regulatory standards. BHCs have long engaged in some form of capital planning to address the expectations of shareholders, creditors, customers, and other stakeholders. The Federal Reserve's interest in and expectations for effective capital planning reflect the importance of the ongoing viability of the largest BHCs even under stressful financial and economic conditions. Even if current assessments of capital adequacy suggest that a BHC's capital level is sufficient to withstand potential economic stress, robust capital planning helps ensure that this outcome will continue to hold in the future. Robust internal capital planning can also help ensure that BHCs have sufficient capital in a broad range of future macroeconomic and financial market environments by governing the capital actions—including dividend payments, share repurchases, and share issuance and conversion—a BHC takes in these situations.

The Federal Reserve's Capital Plan Rule requires all U.S.-domiciled, top-tier BHCs with total consolidated assets of $50 billion or more to develop and maintain a capital plan supported by a robust process for assessing their capital adequacy.[2] CCAR is the Federal Reserve's supervisory program for assessing the capital plans. In 2013, CCAR covered 18 BHCs that participated in the 2009 Supervisory Capital Assessment Program (SCAP).[3] The Federal Reserve's assessment of a BHC's capital planning process includes an evaluation of the risk-identification, -measurement, and -management practices that support the BHC's capital planning and stress scenario analysis, an assessment of stressed loss and revenue estimation practices, and a review of the governance and controls around these practices. The preamble to the Capital Plan Rule outlines the elements on which the Federal Reserve evaluates the robustness of a BHC's internal capital planning—also referred to as the capital adequacy process, or "CAP." These principles are summarized in figure 1.[4]

This publication describes the Federal Reserve's expectations for internal capital planning at the large, complex BHCs subject to the Capital Plan Rule in light of the seven CAP principles. It expands on previous articulations of these supervisory expectations by providing examples of observed practices among the BHCs participating in CCAR 2013 and by highlighting those practices considered to be stronger or leading practices at these firms. In addition, it identi-

---

[1] See SR Letter 12-17, "Consolidated Supervision Framework for Large Financial Institutions," (December 17, 2012), www.federalreserve.gov/bankinforeg/srletters/sr1217.htm; 12 CFR 225.8.

[2] 12 CFR 225.8.

[3] The plans of the remaining BHCs subject to the Capital Plan Rule have been assessed through a separate process (the Capital Plan Review). Beginning in 2014, the capital plans of all BHCs subject to the Capital Plan Rule will be evaluated in a single, unified process through CCAR.

[4] See 76 Fed. Reg. 74631, 74634 (December 1, 2011).

> **Figure 1. Seven principles of an effective capital adequacy process**
>
> **Principle 1: Sound foundational risk management**
>
> The BHC has a sound risk-measurement and risk-management infrastructure that supports the identification, measurement, assessment, and control of all material risks arising from its exposures and business activities.
>
> **Principle 2: Effective loss-estimation methodologies**
>
> The BHC has effective processes for translating risk measures into estimates of potential losses over a range of stressful scenarios and environments and for aggregating those estimated losses across the BHC.
>
> **Principle 3: Solid resource-estimation methodologies**
>
> The BHC has a clear definition of available capital resources and an effective process for estimating available capital resources (including any projected revenues) over the same range of stressful scenarios and environments used for estimating losses.
>
> **Principle 4: Sufficient capital adequacy impact assessment**
>
> The BHC has processes for bringing together estimates of losses and capital resources to assess the combined impact on capital adequacy in relation to the BHC's stated goals for the level and composition of capital.
>
> **Principle 5: Comprehensive capital policy and capital planning**
>
> The BHC has a comprehensive capital policy and robust capital planning practices for establishing capital goals, determining appropriate capital levels and composition of capital, making decisions about capital actions, and maintaining capital contingency plans.
>
> **Principle 6: Robust internal controls**
>
> The BHC has robust internal controls governing capital adequacy process components, including policies and procedures; change control; model validation and independent review; comprehensive documentation; and review by internal audit.
>
> **Principle 7: Effective governance**
>
> The BHC has effective board and senior management oversight of the CAP, including periodic review of the BHC's risk infrastructure and loss- and resource-estimation methodologies; evaluation of capital goals; assessment of the appropriateness of stressful scenarios considered; regular review of any limitations and uncertainties in all aspects of the CAP; and approval of capital decisions.

fies practices that the Federal Reserve deems to be weaker, or in some cases unacceptable, and thus in need of significant improvement. However, practices identified in this publication as leading or industry-best practices should not be considered a safe harbor. The Federal Reserve anticipates that leading practices will continue to evolve as new data become available, economic conditions change, new products and businesses introduce new risks, and estimation techniques advance further.

While the supervisory scenarios and supervisory stress tests that are required under the Dodd-Frank Act[5] play an important role in CCAR,[6] they are not meant to be and should not be viewed as providing for an all-encompassing assessment of the possible risks a BHC may face. A robust internal capital planning process should include modeling practices and scenario assumptions that reflect BHC-specific factors. In certain instances, these practices and assumptions may differ considerably from those used by the Federal Reserve. Indeed, designing an internal capital planning process that simply seeks to mirror the Federal Reserve's stress testing is a weak practice. Many lagging practices identified in this publication involve modeling approaches or BHC stress scenarios that fail to reflect BHC-specific factors or that rely on generic assumptions or "standard" modeling techniques, without sufficient consideration of whether those assumptions or techniques are the most appropriate ones for the BHC.

The supervisory expectations summarized here are broad and reflect, at a general level, the key characteristics of a sound and robust internal capital planning process. While certain aspects of the detailed discussion that follows may be less relevant to individual BHCs based on their business mix and risk

---

[5] 12 CFR part 225, subpart F.
[6] See 12 CFR 225.8(d)(2), 225.8(e)(1).

profile, the core tenets espoused are broadly applicable to all BHCs subject to the Capital Plan Rule.

Importantly, the Federal Reserve has tailored expectations for BHCs of different sizes, scope of operations, activities, and systemic importance in various aspects of capital planning. For example, the Federal Reserve has significantly heightened supervisory expectations for the largest and most complex BHCs—in all aspects of capital planning—and expects these BHCs to have capital planning practices that are widely considered to be leading practices. In addition, the Federal Reserve recognizes the challenges facing BHCs that are new to CCAR and further recognizes that these BHCs will continue to develop and enhance their capital planning systems and processes to meet supervisory expectations.

The purpose of this publication is two-fold. First, it is intended to assist BHC management in assessing their current capital planning processes and in designing and implementing improvements to those processes. Second, it is intended to assist a broader audience in understanding the key aspects of capital planning practices at large, complex U.S. BHCs and the importance the Federal Reserve puts on ensuring that these firms have robust capital resources.

The sections that follow provide greater detail on supervisory expectations and the range of current practice across several dimensions of BHCs' internal capital planning processes. The first section discusses foundational risk management, including identification of risk exposures. The next two sections focus on controls and governance around internal capital planning processes. The fourth section covers expectations and the range of current practice concerning BHCs' capital policies—the internal guidelines governing the capital action decisions made by a BHC under a range of potential future conditions for the firm and for the macroeconomic and financial market environments in which it operates. The subsequent three sections focus on the key elements of BHCs' internal enterprise-wide scenario analysis: design of the stress scenarios and modeling the impact of the scenarios on losses, revenues, balance sheet composition and size, and capital. The final section summarizes the Federal Reserve's conclusions on the current range of practice at BHCs.

Foundational Risk Management

BHCs are expected to have effective risk-identification, -measurement, -management, and -control processes in place to support their internal capital planning.[7] In addition to the assessments of a BHC's stress scenario analysis and stressed loss- and revenue-estimation practices, supervisory assessments of BHCs' internal capital planning will continue to focus on fundamental risk-identification, -measurement, and -management practices, as well as on internal controls and governance. Weaknesses in these areas may contribute to a negative supervisory assessment of a BHC's capital planning process that could lead to an objection to a BHC's capital plan.[8]

A key lesson from the recent financial crisis is that many financial companies simply failed to adequately identify the potential exposures and risks stemming from their firm-wide activities. This was in part a failure of information technology and management information systems (MIS), the often fractured nature of which made it difficult for some companies to identify and aggregate exposures across the firm. But more importantly, many companies failed to consider the full scale and scope of exposures, and to analyze how the size and risk characteristics of their exposures and business activities might evolve as economic and market conditions changed. Combining a comprehensive identification of a firm's business activities and associated positions across the organization with effective techniques for assessing how those positions and activities may evolve under stressful economic and market conditions, and assessing the potential impact of that evolution on the capital needs of the firm, are critical elements of capital planning. A robust internal capital adequacy assessment process relies on the underlying strength of each of these elements.

Risk Identification

BHCs should have risk-identification processes that ensure that all risks are appropriately accounted for when assessing capital needs.[9] These processes should evaluate the full set of potential exposures stemming from on- and off-balance sheet positions, including those that could arise from provisions of non-contractual support to off-balance-sheet entities, and risks conditional on changing economic and financial market conditions during periods of stress. BHCs should have a systematic and repeatable process to identify all risks and consider the potential impact to capital from these risks. In addition, BHCs should closely assess any assumptions about risk reduction resulting from risk transfer and/or mitigation techniques, including, for example, analysis of the enforceability and effectiveness of any guarantees or netting and collateral agreements and the access to and valuation of collateral as exposures and asset values are changing rapidly in a stressed market.

Stronger risk-identification practices include standardized processes through which senior management regularly update risk assessments, review risk exposures and consider how their risk exposures might evolve under a variety of stressful situations. For example, many BHCs maintain a comprehensive inventory of risks to which they are exposed, and refresh it as conditions warrant (such as changes in the business mix and the operating environment) with input from various units across the BHC. Senior representatives from major lines of business, corporate risk management, finance and treasury, and other business and risk functions with perspectives on BHC-wide positions and risks provide input to the process. Consideration of the risks inherent in new products and activities should be a key part of

---

[7] 12 CFR 225.8(d)(2).
[8] 12 CFR 225.8(e)(2).

[9] 12 CFR 225.8(d)(2).

risk-identification and -assessment programs, which should also consider risks that may be associated with any change in the BHC's strategic direction.

Risk measures should be able to capture changes in an institution's risk profile—whether due to a change in the BHC's strategic direction, specific new products, increased volumes, changes in concentration or portfolio quality, or the overall economic environment—on a timely basis. These risk measures should support BHCs' assessments of capital adequacy and may be helpful in capital contingency plans as early warning indicators or contingency triggers, where appropriate.

BHCs should be able to demonstrate how their identified risks are accounted for in their capital planning processes. If certain risks are omitted from the enterprise-wide scenario analysis, BHCs should note how these risks are accounted for in other aspects of the capital planning process (see box 1 for illustration of how BHCs identified and captured certain risks that are more difficult to quantify in their capital planning process). If a BHC employs risk quantification methodologies in its capital planning that are not scenario-based, it should identify which risks each of the methodologies covers, to facilitate comparability and informed decisionmaking with respect to overall capital adequacy. BHCs with lagging practice did not transparently link their evaluation of capital adequacy to the full range of identified risks. These BHCs were not able to show how all their risks were accounted for in their capital planning processes. In some cases, staff responsible for capital planning operated in silos and developed standalone risk inventories not linked to the enterprise-wide risk inventory or to other risk governance functions within their BHCs.

Box 1. Incorporating Risks That Are More Difficult to Quantify

Scenario-based stress testing is a critical element of robust capital planning. However, stress testing based on a limited number of discrete scenarios cannot and is not expected to capture all potential risks faced by a BHC, and therefore, it should serve as one of several inputs to the capital planning process. Given the scope of operations at and the associated breadth of risks facing large, complex BHCs—including the risk of losses from exposures and of reduced revenue generation—they are often exposed to risks, other than credit or market risk, that are either difficult to quantify or not directly attributable to any of the specific integrated firm-wide scenarios that are evaluated as part of the BHC's scenario-based stress testing ("other risks"). Examples of these other risks include reputational risk, strategic risk, and compliance risk. As noted in the section on risk identification, a BHC should identify and assess all risks as part of its risk-identification process and should capture the potential effect of all risks in its capital planning process. A BHC's capital planning process should assess the potential impact of these other risks on the BHC's capital position to ensure that its capital provides a sufficient buffer against all risks to which the BHC is exposed.

There is a wide range of practices around how BHCs account for other risks as part of their capital planning process. Many BHCs used internal capital targets to account for such risks, putting in place an incremental cushion above their targets to allow for difficult-to-quantify risks and the inherent uncertainty represented by any forward-looking capital planning process. Other BHCs assessed the effect of in terms of some combination of reduced revenue, added expenses, or a management overlay on top of loss estimates. BHCs with lagging practices did not even attempt to account for other risks in their capital planning process.

To the extent possible, BHCs should incorporate the effect of these other risks into their projections of net income over the nine-quarter planning horizon. BHCs should clearly articulate and support any relevant assumptions and the methods used to quantify the effect of other risks on their revenue, expenses, or losses.

For those BHCs that did not incorporate the potential impact of these other risks into their capital targets, stronger practices included a clear articulation of which risks were being addressed by putting in place a cushion above the capital target, and how this cushion is related to identified risks. BHCs should clearly support the method they used to measure the potential effect of such risks. Using a simple rule (such as a percent of capital) or expert judgments to determine the cushion above the capital target, without providing analysis or support, is a lagging practice.

Internal Controls

As with other aspects of key risk-management and finance area functions, a BHC should have a strong internal control framework that helps govern its internal capital planning processes. These controls should include (1) regular and comprehensive review by internal audit; (2) robust and independent model review and validation practices; (3) comprehensive documentation, including policies and procedures; and (4) change controls.

Scope of Internal Controls

A BHC's internal control framework should address its entire capital planning process, including the risk measurement and management systems used to produce input data, the models and other techniques used to generate loss and revenue estimates; the aggregation and reporting framework used to produce reports to management and boards; and the process for making capital adequacy decisions. While some BHCs may naturally develop components of their internal capital planning along separate business lines, the control framework should ensure that BHC management reconciles the separate components in a coherent manner. The control framework also should help assure that all aspects of the capital planning process are functioning as intended in support of robust assessments of capital needs.

BHCs with stronger control coverage reviewed the controls around capital planning on an integrated basis and applied them consistently. Management responded quickly and effectively to issues identified by control areas and devoted appropriate resources to continually ensure that controls were functioning effectively.

Internal Audit

Internal audit should play a key role in evaluating internal capital planning and its various components. Audit should perform a review of the full process, not just of the individual components, periodically to ensure that the entire end-to-end process is functioning in accordance with supervisory expectations and with a BHC's board of directors' expectations as detailed in approved policies and procedures. Internal audit should review the manner in which deficiencies are identified, tracked, and remediated. Audit staff should have the appropriate competence and influence to identify and escalate key issues, and the internal audit function should report regularly on the status of all aspects of the capital planning process—including any identified deficiencies related to the BHC's capital plan—to senior management and the board of directors.

BHCs with stronger audit practices provided a comprehensive, robust review of all components of the capital planning process, including all of the control elements noted earlier.[10] BHCs with leading internal audit practices around internal capital planning had strong issue identification and remediation tracking as well. They also ensured that audit staff had strong technical expertise, elevated stature in the organization, and proper independence from management.[11]

Independent Model Review and Validation

BHCs should conduct independent review and validation of all models used in internal capital planning, consistent with existing supervisory guidance on model risk management (SR Letter 11-7).[12] Validation staff should have the necessary technical compe-

---

[10] See 12 CFR 225.8(d)(1)(iii).

[11] See SR Letter 13-1, "Supplemental Policy Statement on the Internal Audit Function and Its Outsourcing," (January 23, 2013) www.federalreserve.gov/bankinforeg/srletters/sr1301.htm, for detailed guidance on expectations for the governance and operational effectiveness of an institution's internal audit function.

[12] See SR Letter 11-7, "Supervisory Guidance on Model Risk Management," (April 4, 2011), www.federalreserve.gov/bankinforeg/srletters/sr1107.htm.

tencies, sufficient stature within the organization, and appropriate independence from model developers and business areas, so that they can provide a critical and unbiased evaluation of the models they review.

The model review and validation process should include

- an evaluation of conceptual soundness;
- ongoing monitoring that includes verification of processes and benchmarking; and
- an "outcomes analysis."

BHCs should maintain an inventory of all models used in the capital planning process, including all input or "feeder" models that produce projections or estimates used by the models that generate the final loss, revenue or expense projections. Consideration should be given to the validity of the use of a model under stressed conditions as models designed for ongoing business activities may be inappropriate for estimating net income and capital under stress conditions. BHCs should also maintain a process to incorporate well-supported adjustments to model estimates when model weaknesses and uncertainties are identified.

BHCs continue to face challenges in conducting outcomes analysis of their stress testing models, given limited realized outcomes against which to assess loss, revenue, or expense projections under stressful scenarios. BHCs should attempt to compensate for the challenges inherent in back-testing stress models by conducting sensitivity analysis or by using benchmark or "challenger" models. BHCs should ensure that validation covers all models and assumptions used for capital planning purposes, including any adjustments management has made to the model estimates (management overlay).

Supervisory reviews have found that, in general, BHCs should give more attention to model risk management, including strengthening practices around model review and validation. Nonetheless, some BHCs exhibited stronger practices in their capital planning, including

- maintaining an updated inventory of all models used in the process;
- ensuring that models had been validated for their intended use; and
- being transparent about the validation status of all models used for capital planning and appropriately addressing any models that had not been validated (or those that had identified weaknesses) by restricting their use, or using benchmark or challenger models to help assess the reasonableness of the primary model output.

BHCs with lagging practices were not able to identify all models used in the capital planning process. They also did not formally review all of the models or assumptions used for capital planning purposes (including some high-impact stress testing models). In addition, they did not have validation staff that were independent and that could critically evaluate the models.

Policies and Procedures

BHCs should ensure they have policies and procedures covering the entire capital planning process.[13] Policies and procedures should ensure a consistent and repeatable process for all components of the capital planning process and provide transparency to third parties regarding this process. Policies should be reviewed and updated at least annually and more frequently when warranted. There should also be evidence that management and staff are adhering to policies and procedures in practice, and there should be a formal process for any policy exceptions. Such exceptions should be rare and approved by the appropriate level of management.

Ensuring Integrity of Results

BHCs should have internal controls that ensure the integrity of reported results and the documentation, review, and approval of all material changes to the capital planning process and its components. A BHC should ensure that such controls exist at all levels of the capital planning process. Specific controls should be in place to

- ensure that MIS are sufficiently robust to support capital analysis and decisionmaking, with sufficient flexibility to run ad hoc analysis as needed;
- provide for reconciliation and data integrity processes for all key reports;
- address the presentation of aggregate, enterprise-wide capital planning results, which should describe any manual adjustments made in the

---

[13] See FR Y-14A reporting form: Summary Schedule Instructions, pp. 5–7.

aggregation process and how those adjustments compensate for identified weaknesses; and

- ensure that reports provided to senior management and the board contain the appropriate level of detail and are accurate and timely. The party responsible for this reporting should assess and report whether the BHC is in compliance with its internal capital goals and targets, and ensure the rationale for any deviations from stated capital objectives is clearly documented and obtain any necessary approvals.[14]

BHCs with stronger practices in this area ensured that good information flows existed to support decisions, with significant investment in controls for data and information. For example, some BHCs had an internal audit group review the data for accuracy and ensured that any data reported to the board and senior management were given extra scrutiny and cross-checking. In addition, BHCs with stronger practices had strong MIS in place that enabled them to collect, synthesize, analyze, and deliver information quickly and efficiently. These systems also had the ability to run ad hoc analysis to support capital planning as needed without employing substantial resources. Other BHCs, however, continue to face challenges with MIS. Many BHCs have systems that are antiquated and/or siloed and not fully compatible, requiring substantial human intervention to reconcile across systems.

Documentation

BHCs should have clear and comprehensive documentation for all aspects of their capital planning processes, including their risk-measurement and risk-management infrastructure, loss- and resource-estimation methodologies, the process for making capital decisions, and efficacy of control and governance functions.[15] Documentation should contain sufficient detail, accurately describe BHCs' practices, allow for review and challenge, and provide relevant information to decisionmakers.[16]

---

[14] See id.

[15] See id.
[16] See id.

Governance

BHCs should have strong board and senior management oversight of their capital planning processes.[17] This includes ensuring periodic review of the BHC's risk infrastructure and loss- and resource-estimation methodologies; evaluation of capital goals and targets; assessment of the appropriateness of stress scenarios considered; regular review of any limitations in key processes supporting internal capital planning, such as uncertainty around estimates; and approval of capital decisions. Together, a BHC's board and senior management should establish a comprehensive capital planning process that fits into broader risk-management processes and that is consistent with the risk-appetite framework and the strategic direction of the BHC.

Board of Directors

A BHC's board of directors has ultimate oversight responsibility and accountability for capital planning and should be in a position to make informed decisions on capital adequacy and capital actions, including capital distributions.[18] The board of directors should receive sufficient information to understand the BHC's material risks and exposures and to inform and support its decisions on capital adequacy and planning. The board should receive this information at least quarterly, or when there are material developments that affect capital adequacy or the manner in which it is assessed. Capital adequacy information provided to the board should include capital measures under current conditions as well as on a post-stress, pro forma basis and should be framed against the capital goals and targets established by the BHC.

The information provided to the board should include sufficient details on scenarios used for the BHC's internal capital planning so that the board can evaluate the appropriateness of the scenarios, given the current economic outlook and the BHC's current risk profile, business activities, and strategic direction. The information should also include a discussion of key limitations, assumptions, and uncertainties within the capital planning process, so that the board is fully informed of any weaknesses in the process and can effectively challenge reported results before making capital decisions. The board should also receive summary information about mitigation strategies to address key limitations and take action when weaknesses in internal capital planning are identified, applying additional caution and conservatism as needed.

BHCs with stronger practices had boards that were informed of and generally understood the risks, exposures, activities, and vulnerabilities that affected the BHC's capital adequacy. They also understood the major drivers of loss and revenue changes under the scenarios used. The boards of BHCs with stronger practices had sufficient expertise and level of engagement to understand and critically evaluate information provided by senior management. Importantly, they recognized that internal capital planning results are estimates and should be viewed as part of a range of possible results. In addition, the boards of BHCs with stronger practices discussed weaknesses identified in the capital planning process, whether they needed to take immediate action to address those weaknesses, and whether the weaknesses were material enough to alter their view of current capital planning results. They also discussed whether a sufficient range of potential stress events and conditions had been considered in assessing capital adequacy.

Board Reporting

The board of directors is required to approve a BHC's capital plan under the Capital Plan Rule.[19] In order for boards to carry out this requirement, management should provide adequate reporting on key

---

[17] See 12 CFR 225.8(d)(1)(iii)(A)–(B).
[18] See 12 CFR 225.8(d)(1)(iii)(C).
[19] Id.

areas of the analysis supporting capital plans. BHCs with stronger practices included information about the independent review and validation of models, information on issues identified by internal audit, as well as key assumptions underpinning stress test results and a discussion of the sensitivity of capital levels to those assumptions. BHCs with stronger practices also supplied their boards with information about past capital planning performance to provide a perspective on how the capital planning process has functioned over time.

BHCs with weaker practices provided insufficient information to the board of directors. For example, at some BHCs, capital distribution recommendations did not include all relevant supporting information and appeared to be based on optimistic expectations about how a given scenario may affect the BHC. In addition, the information did not specifically identify and address key assumptions that supported the capital planning process. In other cases, the board of directors did not receive information about governance and controls over internal capital planning, making it difficult to assess the strength of its capital planning processes and whether results were reliable and credible.

Senior Management

Senior management is responsible for ensuring that capital planning activities authorized by the board are implemented in a satisfactory manner and is accountable to the board for the effectiveness of those activities. Senior management should ensure that effective controls are in place around the capital planning process—including ensuring that the BHC's stress scenarios are sufficiently severe and cover the material risks and vulnerabilities facing the BHC.[20]

Senior management should make informed recommendations to the board of directors about the BHC's capital, including capital goals and distribution decisions. Senior management also should ensure that proposed capital goals have sufficient analytical support and fully reflect the expectations of important stakeholders, including creditors, counterparties, investors, and supervisors. Senior management should identify weaknesses and potential limitations in the capital planning process and evaluate them for materiality. In addition, it should develop remediation plans for any weaknesses affecting the reliability of internal capital planning results. Both the specific identified limitations and the remediation plans should be reported to the board.

Senior management with stronger practices recognized the imprecision and prevalence of uncertainty in predicting future outcomes when reviewing information and results from enterprise-wide scenario analysis. At BHCs with stronger practices, senior management maintained an ongoing assessment of all capital planning areas, identifying and clearly documenting any weaknesses, assumptions, limitations, and uncertainties, and did not consider a one-time assessment of the capital planning process to be sufficient. Furthermore, management developed clear remediation plans with specific timelines for resolving identified weaknesses. In some cases, based on its review of the full capital planning process, senior management made more cautious or conservative adjustments to the capital plan, such as recommending less aggressive capital actions. Management also included key assumptions and process weaknesses in reports and specifically pointed them out to the board, in some cases providing analysis showing the sensitivity of capital to alternative outcomes.

Documenting Decisions

BHCs should document decisions about capital adequacy and capital actions taken by the board of directors and senior management, and describe the information used to reach those decisions.[21] Final decisions regarding capital planning of the board or of a designated committee thereof should be recorded and retained in accordance with the company's policies and procedures.

BHCs with stronger documentation practices had board minutes that described how decisions were made and what information was used. Some documentation provided evidence that the board challenged results and recommendations, including reviewing and assessing how senior management challenged the same information. BHCs with weaker documentation practices had board minutes that were very brief and opaque, with little reference to information used by the board to make its decisions. Some BHCs did not formally document key decisions.

---

[20] 12 CFR 225.8(d)(2)(i)(A)–(D).

[21] See FR Y-14A reporting form: Summary Schedule Instructions, p. 6.

Capital Policy

As noted earlier, a capital policy is the principles and guidelines used by a BHC for capital planning, capital issuance, and usage and distributions. A capital policy should include internal capital goals; quantitative or qualitative guidelines for dividends and stock repurchases; strategies for addressing potential capital shortfalls; and internal governance procedures around capital policy principles and guidelines.[22] The capital policy, as a component of a capital plan, must be approved by the BHC's board of directors or a designated committee of the board.[23] It should be a distinct, comprehensive written document that addresses the major components of the BHC's capital planning processes and links to and is supported by other policies (risk-management, stress testing, model governance, audit, and others). A capital policy should provide details on how a BHC manages, monitors, and makes decisions regarding all aspects of capital planning. The policy should also address roles and responsibilities of decisionmakers, process and data controls, and validation standards. Finally, the capital policy should explicitly lay out expectations for the information included in the BHC's capital plan.

A capital policy should describe targets for the level and composition of capital and provide clarity about the BHC's objectives in managing its capital position. The policy should explain how the BHC's capital planning practices align with the imperative of maintaining a strong capital position and being able to continue to operate through periods of severe stress. It should include quantitative metrics such as common stock dividend (and other) payout ratios as maximums or targets for capital distributions. The policy should include an explanation of how management concluded that these ratios are appropriate, sustainable, and consistent with its capital objectives, business model, and capital plan. It should also specify the capital metrics that senior management and the board use to make capital decisions. In addition, a capital policy should include governance and escalation protocols that are clear, credible, and actionable in the event an actual or projected capital ratio target is breached.

The policy should describe processes surrounding how common stock dividend and repurchase decisions are made and how the BHC arrives at its planned capital distribution amounts. Specifically, the policy should discuss the following:

- the main factors and key metrics that influence the size, timing, and form of capital distributions
- the analytical materials used in making capital distribution decisions (e.g., reports, earnings, stress test results, and others)
- specific circumstances that would cause the BHC to reduce or suspend a dividend or stock repurchase program
- factors the BHC would consider if contemplating the replacement of common equity with other forms of capital
- key roles and responsibilities, including the individuals or groups responsible for producing the analytical material referenced above, reviewing the analysis, making capital distribution recommendations, and making the ultimate decisions

BHCs should establish a minimum frequency (at least annually) and other triggers for when its capital policy is reevaluated and ensure that these triggers remain relevant and current. The capital policy should be reevaluated and revised as necessary to address changes to organizational structure, governance structure, business strategy, capital goals, regulatory environment, risk appetite, and other factors potentially affecting a BHC's capital adequacy. BHCs should develop a formal process for approvals, change management, and documentation retention relating to their capital policies.

Weak capital policies were typically characterized by a limited scope. They only addressed parts of the

---

[22] 12 CFR 225.8(c)(4).
[23] See 12 CFR 225.8(d)(1)(iii)(C), 225.8(d)(2)(iii).

capital planning process, did not provide sufficient detail to convey clearly how capital action decisions will be made, were not well integrated with or supported by other risk and finance policies, and/or did not contain all of the elements described above (e.g., clearly defined capital goals, guidelines for capital distributions and capital composition, etc.). In some cases, the capital policy was overly generic and not tailored to the BHC's unique circumstances. For example, the policy appeared to be restating supervisory expectations without concrete examples or BHC-specific considerations. In other cases, the more detailed procedures were not presented to the board, thus limiting the board's ability to understand the analysis underlying its capital planning decisions.

Capital Goals and Targets

BHCs should establish capital goals aligned with their risk appetites and risk profiles as well as expectations of internal and external stakeholders, providing specific goals for the level and composition of capital, both current and under stressed conditions. Internal capital goals should be sufficient to allow a BHC to continue its operations during and after the impact of stressful conditions. As such, capital goals should reflect current and future regulatory capital requirements, as well as the expectations of shareholders, rating agencies, counterparties, creditors, supervisors, and other stakeholders.

BHCs should also establish capital targets above their capital goals to ensure that capital levels will not fall below the goals during periods of stress. Capital targets should take into consideration forward-looking elements related to the economic outlook, the BHC's financial condition, the potential impact of stress events, and the uncertainty inherent in the capital planning process. The goals and targets should be specified in the capital policy and reviewed and approved by the board.[24]

In developing their capital goals and targets, particularly with regard to setting the levels of capital distributions, BHCs should explicitly take into account general economic conditions and their plans to grow their on- and off-balance-sheet size and risks organically or through acquisitions. BHCs should consider the impact of external conditions during both normal and stressed economic and market environments and other factors on their overall capital adequacy and ability to raise additional capital, including the potential impact of contingent exposures and broader market or systemic events, which could cause risk to increase beyond the BHC's chosen risk-tolerance level. BHCs should have contingency plans for such outcomes.

Additionally, BHCs should calculate and use several capital measures that represent both leverage and risk, including quarterly estimates of regulatory capital ratios (including tier 1 common ratio) under both baseline and stress conditions. BHCs with weaker practices in this area did not clearly link decisions regarding capital distributions to capital adequacy metrics or internal capital goals.

Weak practices observed in this area included establishing capital goals based solely on regulatory minimums and the ratios required to be considered well-capitalized without consideration of a BHC's specific capital needs given its risk profile, financial condition, business model and strategies, overall complexity, and sensitivity to changing conditions. Some BHCs did not recognize uncertainties and limitations in capturing all potential sources of loss and in projecting loss and revenue estimates, which reduced the BHCs' ability to establish effective capital goals and targets. Other BHCs were not transparent about how they determined the capital goals and targets in their capital policies.

Capital Contingency Plan

BHCs should outline in their capital policies specific capital contingency actions they would consider to remedy any current or prospective deficiencies in their capital position.[25] In particular, a BHC's policy should include a detailed explanation of the circumstances—including deterioration in the economic environment, market conditions, or the financial condition of the BHC—in which it will reduce or suspend a dividend or repurchase program or not execute a previously planned capital action. The policy also should define a set of capital triggers and events that would correspond with these circumstances. These triggers should be established for both baseline and stress scenarios and measured against the BHC's capital targets in those scenarios. These triggers and events should be used to guide the frequency with which board and senior management will revisit planned capital actions as well as review

---

[24] 12 CFR 225.8(c)(4).

[25] Id.

and act on contingency capital plans. The capital contingency plan should be reviewed and updated as conditions warrant, such as where there are material changes to the BHC's organizational structure or strategic direction or to capital structure, credit quality, and/or market access.

Capital triggers should provide an "early warning" of capital deterioration and should be part of a management decisionmaking framework, which should include target ranges for a normal operating environment and threshold levels that trigger management action. Such action should include escalation to the board, potential suspension of capital actions, and/or activation of a capital contingency plan. Triggers should also be established for other metrics and events that measure or affect the financial condition or perceived financial condition of the firm—for example, liquidity, earnings, debt and credit default swap spreads, ratings downgrades, stock performance, supervisory actions, or general market stress.

Contingency actions should be flexible enough to work in a variety of situations and be realistic for what is achievable during periods of stress. The capital plan should be prepared recognizing that certain capital-raising and capital-preserving activities may not be feasible or effective during periods of stress. BHCs should have an understanding of market capacity constraints when evaluating potential capital actions that require accessing capital markets, including debt or equity issuance and also contemplated asset sales. Contingency actions should be ranked according to ease of execution and their impact and should incorporate the assessment of stakeholder reactions (e.g., impacts on future capital-raising activities).

Weak capital contingency plans provided few options to address contingency situations and/or did not consider the feasibility of options under stressful conditions. Plans with overly optimistic assumptions or excessive reliance on past history (in terms of both possible contingency situations and options to address those situations) were also considered weak, as were plans that lacked support for the feasibility and availability of possible contingency actions. Other weak practices included establishing triggers based on actual results but not on projected results, or based on minimum regulatory capital ratios only with no consideration of the expectations of other stakeholders including counterparties, creditors and investors, or of other metrics or market indicators.

BHC Scenario Design

Under the Capital Plan Rule, a BHC is required to use a BHC-developed stressed scenario that is appropriate for its business model and portfolios.[26] Accordingly, BHCs should have a process for designing scenarios for enterprise-wide scenario analysis that reflects the BHC's unique business activities and associated vulnerabilities.

The range of observed practice for developing BHC stress scenarios was broad. Some BHCs designed stress scenarios using internal models and expertise. Other BHCs used vendor-defined macroeconomic scenarios or used vendor models to define customized macroeconomic scenarios. For BHCs with internally developed scenarios, those with stronger scenario-design practices used internal models in combination with expert judgment rather than relying solely on either models or expert judgment to define scenario conditions and variables. Among BHCs that used third-party scenarios, those with stronger practices tailored third-party-defined scenarios to their own risk profiles and unique vulnerabilities.

Regardless of the method used to develop the scenario, BHCs should have a scenario-selection process that engages a broad range of internal stakeholders such as risk experts, business managers, and senior management. Although they are required to submit only one BHC stress scenario for CCAR, BHCs should develop a suite of scenarios that collectively capture their material risks and vulnerabilities under a variety of stressful circumstances and should incorporate them into their overall capital planning processes.

Scenario Design and Severity

As indicated in the preamble to the Capital Plan Rule, "the bank holding company-designed stress scenario should reflect an individual company's unique vulnerabilities to factors that affect its firm-wide activities and risk exposures, including macroeconomic, market-wide, and firm-specific events."[27] Thus, BHC stress scenarios should reflect macroeconomic and financial conditions that are tailored specifically to stress a BHC's key vulnerabilities and idiosyncratic risks, based on factors such as its particular business model, mix of assets and liabilities, geographic footprint, portfolio characteristics, and revenue drivers. A BHC stress scenario that simply features a generic weakening of macroeconomic conditions similar in magnitude to the supervisory severely adverse scenario does not meet these expectations.

BHCs with stronger scenario-design practices clearly and creatively tailored their BHC stress scenarios to their unique business-model features, emphasizing important sources of risk not captured in the supervisory severely adverse scenario. Examples of such risks observed in practice included a significant counterparty default; a natural disaster or other operational-risk event; and a more acute stress on a particular region, industry, and/or asset class as compared to the stress applied to general macroeconomic conditions in the supervisory adverse and severely adverse scenarios.

At the same time, BHC stress scenarios should not feature assumptions that specifically benefit the BHC. For example, some BHCs with weaker scenario-design practices assumed that they would be viewed as strong compared to their competitors in a stress scenario and would therefore experience increased market share. Such assumptions are contrary to the supervisory expectations for and the intent of a stress testing exercise that informs capital planning.

While a broad-based recession adversely affects a wide range of most BHCs' business activities, BHCs may have business models or important business

---

[26] 12 CFR 225.8(d)(2)(i)(A).

[27] See 77 *Fed. Reg.* 74631, 74636 (December 1, 2011).

activities that generate vulnerabilities that are not particularly well captured by scenario analysis based on a stressed macroeconomic environment (or for which even a severe recession is not the primary source of potential vulnerability). These BHCs should incorporate into their stress scenarios elements that address the key revenue vulnerabilities and sources of loss for their specific businesses and activities. In combination, the recession incorporated into the BHC stress scenario and any additional elements intended to address specific businesses or activities should result in a substantial stress for the organization, including a significant reduction in capital ratios relative to baseline projections. However, a BHC stress scenario that produces post-stress capital ratios lower than those under the supervisory severely adverse scenario is not, in and of itself, a safe harbor. The stress scenario included in a BHC's capital plan should place substantial strains on its ability to generate revenue and absorb losses, consistent with its unique risks and vulnerabilities.

Variable Coverage

The set of variables that a BHC includes in its stress scenario should be sufficient to address all material risks arising from its exposures and business activities. A business line could face significant stress from multiple sources, requiring more than one risk factor or macroeconomic variable. The scenario should generally contain the relevant variables to facilitate pro forma financial projections that capture the impact of changing conditions and environments. BHCs should have a consistent process for determining the final set of variables and provide this rationale as part of the scenario narrative.

Overall, BHCs with stronger scenario-design practices generated scenarios in which the link between the variables included in the scenario and sources of risk to the BHC's financial outlook were transparent and straightforward. Clear narratives helped make these links more transparent. BHCs with weaker scenario-design practices developed stress scenarios that excluded some variables relevant to the BHC's risk profile and idiosyncratic vulnerabilities. For example, some BHCs with significant trading activities and revenues included a limited set of relevant financial variables. Other BHCs with significant regional and/or industry concentrations did not include relevant geographic or industry variables.

Clear Narratives

The scenario should be supported by a clear narrative describing how the scenario addresses the particular vulnerabilities and material risks facing the BHC. BHCs with stronger scenario-design practices provided narratives describing how the scenario variables related to the risks faced by a BHC's significant business lines and, in some cases, how the scenario variables corresponded to variables in the BHC's internal risk-management models. The narratives also provided explanations of how a scenario stressed a BHC's unique vulnerabilities specific to its business model and how the paths of the scenario variables related to each other in an economically intuitive way. Weaker practices included scenario narratives that did not provide any context for the variable paths as well as scenario narratives that described features that were not reflected in any variables considered in a BHC's internal capital planning.

Estimation Methodologies for Losses, Revenues, and Expenses

A BHC's capital plan must include estimates of projected revenues, expenses, losses, reserves, and pro forma capital levels, including any minimum regulatory capital ratios, the tier 1 common ratio and any additional capital measures deemed relevant by the BHC, over the planning horizon under expected conditions and under a range of stressed scenarios.[28]

General Expectations

Projections of losses, revenues, and expenses under hypothetical stressed conditions serve as the fundamental building blocks of the pro forma financial analysis supporting enterprise-wide scenario analysis. BHCs should have stress testing methodologies that generate credible estimates that are consistent with assumed scenario conditions. It is important for BHCs to understand the uncertainties around their estimates, including the sensitivity of the estimates to changes in inputs and key assumptions. Overall, BHCs' estimates of losses, revenues, and expenses under each of the scenarios should be supported by empirical evidence, and the entire estimation process should be transparent and repeatable. The Federal Reserve generally expects BHCs to use models or other quantitative methods as the basis for their estimates; however, there may be instances where a management overlay or other qualitative approaches may be appropriate due to data limitations, new products or businesses, or other factors. In such instances, BHCs should ensure that such processes are well supported, transparent, and repeatable over time.

Establishing a Quantitative Basis for Enterprise-Wide Scenario Analysis

Generally, BHCs should develop and use internal data to estimate losses, revenues, and expenses as part of enterprise-wide scenario analysis.[29] However, in certain instances, it may be more appropriate for BHCs to use external data to make their models more robust. For example, BHCs may lack sufficient, relevant historical data due to factors such as systems limitations, acquisitions, or new products. When using external data, BHCs should take care to ensure that the external data reasonably approximate underlying risk characteristics of their portfolios, and make adjustments to modeled outputs to account for identified differences in risk characteristics and performance reflected in internal and external data.

BHCs can use a range of quantitative approaches to estimate losses, revenues, and expenses, depending on the type of portfolio or activity for which the approach is used, the granularity and length of available time series of data, and the materiality of a given portfolio or activity. While the Federal Reserve does not require BHCs to use a specific estimation method, each BHC should estimate its losses, revenues, and expenses at sufficient granularity so that it can identify common, key risk drivers and capture the effect of changing conditions and environments. For example, loss models should be estimated at a sufficiently granular subportfolio or segment level so that they can capture observed variations in risk characteristics and performance across the subportfolios or segments and across time, and account for changing exposure or portfolio characteristics over the planning horizon.

While BHCs often segment their portfolios and activities along functional areas, such as by line of business or product type, the leading practice is to determine segments based on common risk characteristics (e.g., credit score ranges or loan-to-value ratio ranges) that exhibit meaningful differences in historical performance. The granularity of segments typically depends on the type, size, and composition of the BHC's portfolio. For example, a more diverse portfolio—both in terms of borrower risk character-

---

[28] 12 CFR 225.8(d)(1).
[29] BHCs are required to collect and report a substantial amount of risk information to the Federal Reserve on FR Y-14 schedules.

These data may help to support the BHCs' enterprise-wide scenario analysis.

istics and performance—would generally require a greater number of segments to account for the heterogeneity of the portfolio. However, when segmenting portfolios, it is important to ensure that each risk segment has sufficient data observations to produce reliable model estimates.

As a general practice, BHCs should separately estimate losses, revenues, or expenses for portfolios or business lines that are sensitive to different risk drivers or sensitive to risk drivers in a markedly different way. For instance, losses on commercial and industrial loans and commercial real estate (CRE) loans are, in part, driven by different factors, with the path of property values having a more pronounced effect on CRE loan losses. Similarly, although falling property value affects both income-producing CRE loans and construction loans, the effect often differs materially due to structural differences between the two portfolios. Such differences can become more pronounced during periods of stress. BHCs with leading practices have demonstrated clearly the rationale for selecting certain risk drivers over others. BHCs with lagging practices used risk drivers that did not have a clear link to results, either statistically or conceptually.

Many models used for stress testing require a significant number of assumptions to implement. Further, the relationship between macroeconomic variables and losses, revenues, or expenses could differ considerably in the hypothetical stress scenario from what is observed historically. As a result, while traditional tools for evaluating model performance (such as comparing projections to historical out-of-sample outcomes) are still useful, the Federal Reserve expects BHCs to supplement them with other types of analysis. Sensitivity analysis is one tool that some BHCs have used to test the robustness of models and to help model developers, BHC management, the board of directors, and supervisors identify the assumptions and parameters that materially affect outcomes. Sensitivity analysis can also help ensure that core assumptions are clearly linked to outcomes. Using results from different estimation approaches (challenger models) as a benchmark is another way BHCs can gain greater comfort around their primary model estimates, as the strengths of one approach could potentially compensate for the weaknesses of another. When using multiple approaches, however, it is important that BHCs have a consistent framework for evaluating the results of different approaches and supporting rationale for why they chose the methods and estimates they ultimately used.

In certain instances, BHCs may need to rely on third-party models—for example, due to limitations in internal modeling capacity. In using these third-party models (vendor models or consultant-developed models), BHCs should ensure that their internal staff have working knowledge and a good conceptual understanding of the design and functioning of the models and potential model limitations so that management can clearly communicate them to those governing the process. An off-the-shelf vendor model often requires some level of firm-specific analysis and customization to demonstrate that it produces estimates appropriate for the BHC and consistent with scenario conditions. Sensitivity analysis can be particularly helpful in understanding the range of possible results of vendor models with less transparent or proprietary elements. Importantly, all vendor and consultant-developed models should be validated in accordance with SR 11-7 guidelines.[30]

Some BHCs generated annual projections for certain loss, revenue, or expense items and then evenly distributed them over the four quarters of each year. This practice does not reflect a careful estimate of the expected quarterly path of losses, net revenue, and capital, and thus is only acceptable when a BHC can clearly demonstrate that the projected item is highly uncertain and the practice likely results in a conservative estimate.

Qualitative Projections, Expert Judgment, and Adjustments

While quantitative approaches are important elements of enterprise-wide scenario analysis, BHCs should not rely on weak or poorly specified models simply to have a modeled approach. In fact, most BHCs use some forms of expert judgment for some purposes—generally as a management adjustment overlay to modeled outputs. And BHCs can, in limited cases, use expert judgment as the primary method to produce an estimate of losses, revenue, or expenses. BHCs may use a management overlay to account for the unique risks of certain portfolios that are not well captured in their models, or otherwise to compensate for specific model and data limitations. Material changes in BHCs' businesses or limitations in relevant data may lead some BHCs to rely wholly on expert judgment for certain loss, revenue, or expense projections. In using expert judgment, BHCs

---

[30] See SR Letter 11-7, "Supervisory Guidance on Model Risk Management," (April 4, 2011), www.federalreserve.gov/bankinforeg/srletters/sr1107.htm.

should ensure that they have a transparent and repeatable process, that management judgments are well supported, and that key assumptions are consistent with assumed scenario conditions.

As with quantitative methods, the assumptions and processes that support qualitative approaches should be clearly documented so that an external reviewer can follow the logic and evaluate the reasonableness of the outcomes.[31] Any potential shortcomings should be investigated and communicated to decisionmakers. In addition, any management overlay or qualitatively derived projections should be subject to effective review and challenge. BHCs should evaluate a range of potential estimates and conduct sensitivity analysis for key assumptions used in the estimation process. For example, if a BHC makes extensive adjustments to its modeled estimates of losses, revenue, and expenses, the impact of such adjustments should be quantified relative to unadjusted estimates, and these results should be documented and made available to BHC management and the board of directors. Finally, extensive use of management judgment to adjust modeled estimates should trigger review and discussion as to whether new or improved modeling approaches are needed. In reporting to the board of directors, management should always provide both the initial results and the results after any judgmental adjustments.

Conservatism and Credibility

Given the uncertainty inherent in a forward-looking capital planning exercise, the Federal Reserve expects BHCs to apply generally conservative assumptions throughout the stress testing process to ensure appropriate tests of the BHCs' resilience to stressful conditions. In particular, BHCs should ensure that models are developed using data that contain sufficiently adverse outcomes. If a BHC experienced better-than-average performance during previous periods of stress, it should not assume that those prior patterns will remain unchanged in the stress scenario. BHCs should carefully review the applicability of key assumptions and critically assess how historically observed patterns may change in unfavorable ways during a period of severe stress for the economy, the financial markets, and the BHC.

In the context of CCAR loss and revenue estimates, BHCs should generally include all applicable loss events in their analysis, unless a BHC no longer engages in a line of business or its activities have changed such that the BHC is no longer exposed to a particular risk. BHCs should not selectively exclude losses based on arguments that the nature of the ongoing business or activity has changed—for example, because certain loans were underwritten to standards that no longer apply or were acquired and, therefore, differ from those that would have been originated by the acquiring institution.

Similarly, BHCs should not rely on favorable assumptions that cannot be reasonably assured to occur in stressed environments given the high level of uncertainty around market conditions. BHCs should also not assume any foresight of scenario conditions over the projection horizon beyond what would reasonably be knowable in real-life situations. For example, some BHCs have used the path of stress scenario variables to make optimistic assumptions about possible management actions *ex ante* in anticipation of stressful conditions, such as preemptively rebalancing their portfolios or otherwise adjusting their risk profiles to mitigate the expected impact. In the event of a downturn, the future path or progression of economic and market conditions would not be clearly known, and this uncertainty should be reflected in the capital plans.

Documentation of Estimation Practices

The Federal Reserve expects BHCs to clearly document their key methodologies and assumptions used to estimate losses, revenues, and expenses.[32] BHCs with stronger practices provided documentation that concisely explained methodologies, with relevant macroeconomic or other risk drivers, and demonstrated relationships between these drivers and estimates. Documentation should clearly delineate among model outputs, qualitative overlays to model outputs, and purely qualitative estimates.[33] BHCs with weaker practices often had limited documentation that was poorly organized and that relied heavily on subjective management judgment for key model inputs with limited empirical support for and documentation of these adjustments.

---

[31] See FR Y-14A reporting form: Summary Schedule Instructions, pp. 5–6.

[32] See id.
[33] See id.

Loss-Estimation Methodologies

As noted earlier, a BHC's internal stress testing processes should be designed to capture risks inherent in its own exposures and business activities. Consistent with any good modeling practices, when developing loss-estimation methodologies, BHCs should first determine whether there is a sound theoretical basis for macroeconomic and other explanatory variables (risk drivers) used to estimate losses, and then empirically demonstrate that a strong relationship exists between those variables and losses. For example, most BHCs' residential-mortgage loss models used some measure of unemployment and a house price index as explanatory variables, which affect a borrower's ability and incentive to repay.

Beyond the core set of macroeconomic variables that typically represents a given scenario, such as gross domestic products (GDP), unemployment rate, Treasury yields, credit spreads, and various price indices, BHCs often project additional variables that have a more direct link to particular portfolios or exposures. Some examples of these variables include regional macroeconomic variables that better capture the BHC's geographic exposures and sector-specific variables, such as office vacancy rates and corporate profits. Using these additional variables to estimate the model can enhance the sensitivity of loss estimates to a given scenario and also improve the overall fit of the model. Any models used to produce additional risk drivers are key components of the loss-estimation process and, therefore, should be included in BHCs' model inventories and receive the same model risk-management treatment as core loss-estimation models.

Generally, BHCs sum up losses from various portfolios and activities to produce aggregate losses for the enterprise-wide scenario analysis. BHCs should have a repeatable process to aggregate losses, particularly when they transform model estimates to combine disparate risk measures (such as accounting-based and economic loss concepts), different measurement horizons, or otherwise dissimilar loss estimates.

BHCs with leading practices used automated processes that showed a clear audit trail from source data to loss estimation and aggregation, with full reconcilement to source systems and regulatory reports and mechanisms requiring approval and logging of judgmental adjustments and overrides. These systems often leveraged existing enterprise-wide financial and regulatory consolidation processes.

BHCs with lagging practices exhibited a high degree of manual intervention in the aggregation process, and applied aggregate-level management adjustments that were not transparent or well supported.

Retail and Wholesale Credit Risk

BHCs used a range of approaches to produce loss estimates on loans to retail and corporate customers, often using different estimation methods for different portfolios. This section describes the observed range of practice for the methods used to project losses on retail and wholesale loan portfolios.

Data and Segmentation

Sources of data used for loss estimation have often differed between retail and wholesale portfolios. Due to availability of a richer set of retail loss data, particularly from the most recent downturn, BHCs generally used internal data to estimate defaults or losses on retail portfolios and only infrequently used external data with longer history to benchmark estimated losses on portfolios that had more limited loss experience in the recent downturn. For wholesale portfolios, some BHCs supplemented internal data with external data or used external data to calibrate their models due to a short time series (5–10 years) that included only a single downturn cycle.

BHCs with stronger practices accounted for dynamic changes in their portfolios, such as loan modifications or changes in portfolio risk characteristics, and made appropriate adjustments to data or estimates to compensate for known data limitations (including lack of historical periods of stress).

BHCs with weaker practices failed to compensate for data limitations or adequately demonstrate that external data reasonably reflect the BHC's actual exposures, often failing to capture geographic, industry, or lending-type concentrations.

The level of segmentation used for modeling varied depending on the type and size of portfolio and estimation methods used. For example, BHCs often segmented the retail portfolio based on some combinations of product; lien position; risk characteristics such as credit score, loan-to-value ratio, and collateral; and underlying collateral information (e.g., single-family home versus condominium), though some models were estimated at the loan-level and others at the portfolio level.

BHCs with stronger practices had segmentation schemes that were well supported by the BHC's data and analysis, with sufficient granularity to capture exposures that react differently to risk drivers under stressed conditions.

BHCs with weaker practices used a single model for multiple portfolios, without sufficiently adjusting modeling assumptions to capture the unique risk drivers of each portfolio. For example, in estimating losses on wholesale portfolios, these BHCs did not adequately allow for variation in loss rates commonly attributed to industry, obligor type, collateral, lien position, or other relevant information.

Common Credit Loan Loss-Estimation Approaches

BHCs have used a wide range of methods to estimate credit losses, depending on the type and size of portfolios and data availability. These methods can be based on either an accounting-based loss approach (that is, charge-off and recovery) or an economic loss approach (that is, expected losses). BHCs have flexibility in selecting a specific loss or estimation approach; however, it is important for BHCs to understand differences between the two loss approaches, particularly in terms of the timing of loss recognition, and to account for the differences in setting the appropriate level of reserves at the end of each quarter.

Expected Loss Approaches

Under the expected loss approach, losses are estimated as a function of three components—probability of default (PD), loss given default (LGD), and exposure at default (EAD). PD, LGD, and EAD can be estimated at a segment level or at an individual loan level, and using different models or assumptions. In general, BHCs used econometric models to estimate losses under a given scenario, where the estimated PDs were conditioned on the macroeconomic environment and portfolio or loan characteristics. Some BHCs used other approaches, such as rating transition models, to estimate stressed default rates as part of an expected loss framework.

BHCs with leading practices were able to break down losses into PD, LGD, and EAD components, separately identifying key risk drivers for each of those components, though they typically did not demonstrate this level of granularity consistently across all portfolios. For certain wholesale portfolios, some BHCs used long-run average PD, LGD, and EAD for a particular segment, such as a rating grade, to estimate losses. By design, estimates based on long-run average behavior over a mix of conditions, including periods of economic expansion and downturn, are not appropriate for projecting losses under stress and should not be used for these purposes.

BHCs with leading practices clearly tied LGD to underlying risk drivers, accounted for collateral and guarantees, and also incorporated the likelihood of a decline in collateral values under stress. However, most BHCs have more limited data on LGD and, as a result, BHCs often applied a simple, conservative assumption (e.g., 100 percent LGD for credit cards), based stressed LGD on their experience during the crisis, or scaled up the historical average LGD using expert judgment. In using such methods, it is important for BHCs to ensure that the process is well supported and transparent in line with the Federal Reserve's general expectation for expert judgment-based estimates. Wherever possible, BHCs should benchmark their estimates with external data or research and analysis.

BHCs with lagging practices modeled LGD using a weighted-average approach at an aggregate portfolio level, without some level of segmentation (e.g., by lending product, priority of claim, collateral type, geography, vintage, or LTV). Or, they failed to demonstrate that LGD estimates were consistent with the severity of the scenario.

Although some BHCs found a relationship between EAD and credit quality, most BHCs did not model EADs to vary according to the macroeconomic environment, in large part due to data limitations. Rather, many BHCs applied a static assumption to estimate stressed EAD.

BHCs with stronger practices included the use of loan equivalent calculations (i.e., estimated additional drawdowns as a percentage of unused commitments, which are added to the outstanding or drawn balance) and credit-conversion factors (i.e., additional drawdowns during the period leading up to default—usually one year prior—as a percentage of both drawn and undrawn commitments) to capture losses associated with undrawn commitments.

BHCs with weaker practices did not project stressed exposures associated with undrawn commitments and/or relied on the assumption that they can actively manage down committed lines during stress scenarios.

Rating Transition Models

Many BHCs have used a rating transition-based approach to produce a stressed rating transition matrix for each quarter, which is then used to estimate losses for their wholesale portfolios under stress. These approaches used credit ratings applied to individual loans by the BHC and projected how these ratings would change over time given the macroeconomic scenario. Although the details of techniques used to link rating transitions to scenario conditions varied across firms, the process usually involved the following steps: (1) converting the rating transition matrix into a single summary measure; (2) estimating a time-series model linking the summary measure to scenario variables; (3) projecting the summary measure over the nine-quarter planning horizon, using the parameter estimates from the time-series model; and (4) converting the projected summary measure into a full set of quarterly transition matrices. BHCs using such an approach should be able to demonstrate that the summary measure responds to changes in economic conditions as expected (that is, worsens as the economic condition deteriorates) and results in projected rating transition matrices that are consistent with the severity of scenario. Judgmentally selecting transition matrices from past stress periods is a weak practice, as it may produce loss estimates that are not consistent with a given scenario and fails to recognize that conditions in the future may not precisely mirror conditions observed by the BHC in the past.

Sound rating transition models require two fundamental building blocks: a robust time series of data and well-calibrated, granular-risk rating systems. The Federal Reserve expects BHCs that use rating transition models to have robust time series of data that include a sufficient number of transitions, which allows BHCs to establish a statistically significant relationship between the transition behavior and macroeconomic variables. Data availability has been a widespread constraint inhibiting the development of granular transition models because a sufficient number of upgrades and downgrades are necessary to preclude sparse matrices. In order to overcome these data limitations, BHCs have often relied on third-party data to develop rating transition models. Consistent with the Federal Reserve's general expectations, when using third-party data, BHCs should be able to demonstrate that the transition matrices estimated with external data are a reasonable proxy for the migration behavior of their portfolios. Rating transition models also require granular ratings systems that capture differences in the potential for defaults and losses for a given set of exposures in various economic environments. BHCs that lack well-calibrated, granular credit-risk rating systems are often unable to produce useful transition matrices.

BHCs with stronger practices typically had more granular ratings system and accounted for limitations in their data and/or credit rating systems by making adjustments to model assumptions or estimates, or by supplementing internal data with external data.

BHCs with weaker practices often failed to demonstrate that supplemented external data adequately reflected the ratings performance of the BHC's portfolio. BHCs with weaker practices also sometimes relied on a risk rating process that historically resulted in lumpiness in rating upgrades and downgrades or material concentrations in one or two rating categories. As a result, these BHCs often produced transition matrices with limited sensitivity to scenario variables, and resulting estimates were more consistent with long-term average default rates than with default rates that would be experienced under severe economic stress.

Roll-Rate Models

Many BHCs have used roll-rate models to estimate losses for various retail portfolios. Roll-rate models generally estimate the rate at which loans that are current or delinquent in a given quarter roll into delinquent or default status in the next period. As a result, they are conceptually similar to rating transition models. The Federal Reserve expects BHCs that use roll-rate models to have a robust time series of data with sufficient granularity. The robust time series data allow the BHC to establish a strong relationship between roll rates and scenario variables, while the availability of granular data enables BHCs to model all relevant loan transitions and to segment the portfolio into subportfolios that exhibit meaningful variations in performance, particularly during the period of stress. In general, BHCs should estimate roll rates using models that are conditioned on scenario variables. For certain transition states where statistical relationships between roll rates and scenarios are weak (such as late stage loan delinquency), BHCs should incorporate conservative assumptions rather than relying solely on statistical relationships.

While roll-rate models have some advantages, including transparency and ease of use, they often have a weak predictive power outside the near future, particularly if they are not properly conditioned on scenario variables. As a result, some roll-rate models have limited usefulness for stress testing over a longer horizon, such as the nine-quarter planning horizon required in CCAR. Some BHCs have used roll-rate models in conjunction with other estimation approaches (such as a vintage model described below) that project losses for later periods. In general, it is a weaker practice to combine two different models, as it can introduce unexpected jumps in estimated losses over the planning horizon, though some BHCs have judgmentally weighed two different estimation methods to smooth projected losses. If BHCs combine two models, they should be able to demonstrate that such an approach is empirically warranted based on output analysis, including sensitivity analysis, and that the process of transitioning from one set of results to the other is consistent, well supported, and transparent.

Vintage Loss Models

Some BHCs use vintage loss models, also known as age-cohort-time models, to estimate losses for certain retail portfolios. BHCs that use vintage loss models generally segment their retail portfolios by vintage and collateral- or credit-quality-based segments. Losses are estimated using a multistep process—developing a baseline seasoning curve for each segment and using a regression model to estimate sensitivity of losses to macroeconomic variables at each seasoning level (e.g., four quarters after origination). This technique is commonly used in several vendor models, but BHCs also have developed and used proprietary models using this technique.

These models have several advantages (such as natural segmentation of portfolio by cohort and maturity) and ease of application to credit products (such as auto loans) that exhibit lifecycle effects. However, vintage models can be very challenging to construct, calibrate, and validate. In particular, it may be difficult to separately identify vintage effects from the effects of macroeconomic variables, which can result in poorly specified models. These models also assume that different cohorts will experience similar losses over time, generating results that are representative of average years, rather than during the period of stress. In using vintage models, it is important for a BHC to be able to demonstrate that the approach appropriately reflects its portfolio composition and history, and that modeled outputs are consistent with stressed conditions.

Charge-Off Models

A minority of BHCs have used net charge-off (NCO) models as either a primary loss-estimation model or a benchmark model. Typically, the NCO models BHCs used estimated a statistical relationship between charge-off rates and macroeconomic variables at a portfolio level, and often included autoregressive terms (lagged NCO rates). While some BHCs also incorporated variables that describe the underlying risk characteristics of the portfolio, NCO models that BHCs used for capital planning generally did not capture variation in sensitivities to risk drivers across important portfolio segments nor accounted for changes in portfolio risk characteristics over time. As a matter of general practice, BHCs should not use models that do not capture changes in portfolio risk characteristics over time and in scenarios used for stress testing as part of their internal capital planning.

NCO models often exhibit lower explanatory power than models that consider distinct portfolio risk drivers. In addition, NCO models implicitly assume that historical charge-off performance is a good predictor of future performance; however, the historical relationship between charge-offs and macro variables may not be realized under very stressful scenarios that fall outside the portfolio's actual historical experience. Accordingly, a NCO model that is estimated without using sufficient segmentation or does not account for current or changing portfolio composition is unlikely to produce robust loss estimates. Thus, BHCs should avoid using such a NCO model as the primary loss-estimation approach for a material portfolio.

Scalar Adjustments

Some BHCs have used simple scalars to adjust portfolio loss estimate under a baseline scenario upward for stress scenarios. Scalars have been calibrated based on some combination of historical performance, the ratio of modeled stressed losses to baseline losses estimated for other portfolios, and expert judgment. Scalar adjustments are easy to develop, implement, and communicate; however, the approach has significant shortcomings, including lack of transparency and lack of sensitivity to changes in portfolio composition and scenario variables. Consequently, the use of these types of approaches should be, at most, limited to immaterial portfolios.

Available-for-Sale (AFS) and Held-to-Maturity (HTM) Securities

BHCs should test all credit-sensitive AFS and HTM securities for potential other-than-temporary impairment (OTTI) regardless of current impairment status. The threshold for determining OTTI for structured products should be based on cash-flow analysis and credit analysis of underlying obligors. Most BHCs used a ratings-based approach to determine OTTI of direct obligations such as corporate bonds, based on the projection of ratings migration under a stress scenario and a ratings-based OTTI threshold. However, some BHCs with weaker practice used a ratings-based approach that kept the ratings static over the scenario horizon.

BHCs should have quantitative methods that capture appropriate risk drivers and explicitly translate assumed scenario conditions into estimated losses. Estimation methods should generate results that conform to standard accounting treatment, are consistent with scenario conditions, and are appropriately sensitive to changes in key variables. Any assumptions (e.g., assumptions related to loss recognition) should be consistent with the intent of a stress testing exercise. Additionally, models should be independently validated for their use in projecting OTTI losses for specific classes of securities.

OTTI processes for AFS and HTM securities portfolios varied in sophistication across BHCs. BHCs with leading practices used estimation methods that capture both security-specific and country-specific performance data for relevant portfolios. For securitized products, they modeled the credit risk of underlying exposures (e.g., commercial real estate loans) to estimate potential losses. Where BHCs used management judgment, it was limited and well supported in the methodology documentation.

In addition, BHCs with leading practices chose conservative approaches and assumptions for OTTI loss estimation, such as recognizing losses in early quarters rather than over the entire scenario horizon. Though, under current accounting rules, OTTI losses are recognized only up to the amount of unrealized losses, some BHCs have taken a conservative approach to allow OTTI losses to exceed projected unrealized losses.

BHCs with lagging practices did not test all credit-sensitive securities for potential OTTI; rather, they tested only currently impaired positions or securities that met a certain criteria (e.g., only securities rated below investment grade) for OTTI. BHCs should not rely solely on a ratings-based threshold to determine OTTI for structured products. BHCs with lagging practices had OTTI loss-estimation methodologies that did not capture appropriate risk drivers or scenario conditions and/or were not applied at a sufficiently granular level. In some cases, BHCs excluded key explanatory variables for certain asset classes. For example, the unemployment rate was used to project OTTI losses for non-agency residential mortgage-backed securities (RMBS), but the housing price index (HPI) was excluded even though the theory and empirical evidence points to a strong relationship between mortgage losses and housing prices. As a result of these methodology deficiencies, these BHCs projected OTTI losses that were inconsistent with the risk characteristics of the portfolio and assumed scenario conditions.

Operational Risk

Best practices in operational-risk models are still evolving, and the Capital Plan Rule does not require BHCs to use advanced measurement approach (AMA) models for stressed operational-risk loss estimation.[34] However, BHCs that have developed a rich set of data to support the AMA should consider leveraging the same data and risk-management tools to estimate operational losses under a stress scenario, regardless of a particular methodology they choose to estimate losses.

Most operational-risk models use historical data on operational-risk loss "events"—incidences in which a BHC has experienced a loss or been exposed to loss due to inadequate or failed internal processes, people, or systems or from external events. Generally, operational-risk events are grouped into one of several event-type categories, such as internal fraud, external fraud, or damage to physical assets.[35] In general, BHCs should use internal operational-loss data

---

[34] 12 CFR part 225, appendix G.

[35] For example, the seven event-type categories used for AMA are internal fraud; external fraud; employment practices and workplace safety; clients, products, and business practices; damage to physical assets; business disruption and system failures; and execution, delivery, and process management.

as a starting point to provide historical perspective, and then incorporate forward-looking elements, idiosyncratic risks, and tail events to estimate losses. Most BHCs have supplemented their internal loss data with external data when modeling operational-risk loss estimates and scaled the losses to make the external loss data more commensurate with their individual risk profiles. The Federal Reserve expects such scaling approaches to be well supported. Few BHCs have incorporated business environment and internal control factors such as risk control self-assessments and other risk indicators into their operational-risk methodology. While the Federal Reserve does not expect BHCs to use these qualitative tools as direct inputs in a model, they can help identify areas of potential risk and help BHCs select appropriate scenarios that stress those risks.

Internal Data Collection and Data Quality

The Federal Reserve expects BHCs to have a robust and comprehensive internal data-collection method that captures key elements, such as critical dates (i.e., occurrence, discovery, and accounting), event types, and business lines. In general, BHCs should use complete data sets of internal losses when modeling, and not judgmentally exclude certain loss data.

Data quality and comprehensiveness have varied considerably across BHCs. BHCs with lagging practices often excluded certain internal loss data from model input for various reasons. Examples include

- excluding large items such as legal reserves and tax/compliance penalties;
- omitting losses from merged or acquired institutions mergers or acquisitions due to complications in collection and aggregation; and
- excluding loss data from discontinued business lines, even though the loss events were reasonably generic and applicable to remaining business lines within the organization.

Some BHCs have addressed observed outliers by omitting them from the data set, modeling them separately, or applying an add-on based on scenario analysis or management input. If BHCs do not have the data from potential mergers and acquisitions, one way to account for this limitation is to scale existing internal data using the size of operations and apply an add-on to applicable business lines or units of measure. If a BHC excludes data or uses data-smoothing techniques, especially as they affect large losses, it should have a well-supported rationale for doing so, and clearly document the rationale and the process.[36]

The Federal Reserve expects BHCs to segment their loss data into units of measure that are granular enough to capture similar losses while balancing it with the availability of data. Most BHCs have segmented datasets by event type; however, some BHCs have segmented the loss data by consolidated business lines, event types, or some combination of the two.

Correlation with Macroeconomic Factors

Most BHCs have attempted to identify correlation between macroeconomic factors and operational-risk losses, but some have struggled to identify a clear relationship for some types of operational-risk loss events. BHCs that did not identify a significant correlation typically developed other methodologies, such as scenario analysis layered onto modeled results, to project stressed operational-risk losses. These approaches can be reasonable alternatives if BHCs can demonstrate that their approach results in sufficiently conservative loss estimates that are consistent with the stress scenario.

BHCs that identified correlations between macroeconomic factors and operational-risk elements typically had large data sets and often used external loss data to supplement internal data. These BHCs often identified correlations between loss frequency and macroeconomic factors for certain event types and adjusted the frequency distributions for the respective event type accordingly.

Common Operational-Loss-Estimation Approaches

Most BHCs have used their annual budgeting or forecasting process to estimate operational losses in the baseline scenario. The process typically uses a combination of historical loss data and management input at a business-line level. Some BHCs have used historical averages from internal loss data to estimate losses in the baseline scenario.

BHCs with stronger practices used a combination of approaches to incorporate historical loss experience, forward-looking elements, and idiosyncratic risks into their stressed loss projections. Using a combination of approaches can help address model and data

---

[36] See FR Y-14A reporting form: Summary Schedule Instructions, p. 5.

limitations. Some BHCs used separate models for certain events types such as fraud or litigation, and used other approaches (e.g., using historical averages) for event types where no correlation with macroeconomic factors was identified. A simple approach may be acceptable depending on the size and complexity of the BHC as well as data and sophistication of models available to them. Very few BHCs have yet developed benchmarks to either challenge or further support the projections provided by their main models.

Regression Models

Most BHCs have used a regression model, either by itself or with another approach described below, to estimate operational-risk losses for stress scenarios. Some BHCs also have used a regression model for the baseline scenarios, albeit with different parameters. Operational-risk regression models are generally used to estimate two variables: loss frequency (i.e., the number of operational-risk losses) and loss severity (i.e., the loss amount).

BHCs that were able to identify significant correlation between macroeconomic variables and operational-risk losses have used regression models to stress the loss frequency or total operational-risk losses. Some macroeconomic variables were adjusted for the purpose of correlation analysis or to reflect time-lag assumptions. Most BHCs judgmentally chose time periods for estimation and model specification rather than justifying them with statistical evidence.

Most BHCs were not able to find meaningful correlation between macroeconomic variables and operational-risk loss severity. As a result, BHCs that used a regression model to estimate loss frequency typically applied the loss-severity assumption (e.g., static or four-quarter moving average) based on the most recent crisis period to estimate operational losses.

Modified Loss-Distribution Approach (LDA)

The LDA is an empirical modeling technique commonly used by BHCs subject to the AMA to estimate annual value-at-risk (VaR) measures for operational-risk losses based on loss data and fitted parametric distributions. The LDA involves estimating probability distributions for the frequency and the severity of operational loss events for each defined unit of measure, whether it is a business line, an event type, or some combination of the two. The estimated frequency and severity distributions are then combined, generally using a Monte Carlo simulation, to estimate the probability distribution for annual operational-risk losses at each unit of measure.

For purposes of CCAR, LDA models have generally been used in one of two ways: (1) by using a lower confidence interval than the 99.9th percentile used by the AMA, or (2) by adjusting the frequency based on outcomes of correlation analysis. BHCs that modified the LDA by using a lower confidence interval typically have used either the mean or median for the baseline estimates and higher confidence intervals—typically ranging from 70th percentile to 98th percentile—for the stressed estimates. Additionally, some BHCs have used different confidence intervals for different event types. The Federal Reserve does not require BHCs to use a particular percentile to produce stressed estimates. However, it expects BHCs to implement a credible, transparent process to select a percentile; be able to demonstrate why the percentile is an appropriate choice given the specific scenario under consideration; and perform sensitivity analyses around the selection of a percentile to test the impact of this assumption on model outputs. Some BHCs modified the LDA by adjusting frequency distributions based on the observed correlation between macroeconomic variables and operational-risk losses.

Scenario Analysis

Scenario analysis is a systematic process of obtaining opinions from business managers and risk-management experts to assess the likelihood and loss impact of plausible severe operational-loss events. Some BHCs have used this process to determine a management overlay that is added to losses estimated using a model-based approach. BHCs have used this overlay to incorporate idiosyncratic risks (particularly for event types where correlation was not identified) or to capture potential loss events that the BHC had not previously experienced. BHCs should be able to demonstrate the quantitative effect of the management overlay on final loss estimates.

Scenario analysis, if used effectively, can help compensate for data and model limitations, and allows BHCs to capture a wide range of risks, particularly where limited data are available. The Federal Reserve expects BHCs using scenario analysis to have a clearly defined process and provide an appropriate rationale for the specific scenarios included in their loss estimate. The process for choosing scenarios should be credible, transparent, and well supported.

Historical Averages

Some BHCs used historical averages of operational-risk losses, in combination with other approaches noted above, to estimate operational-risk losses under stress scenarios. For example, BHCs have used historical averages for event types where no correlation between macroeconomic factors and operational-risk losses was identified but used a regression model for event types where correlations were identified. A small number of BHCs have used historical averages as the sole approach to develop stressed loss estimates. When used alone, this approach is backward-looking and excludes potential risks the BHCs have not experienced. When using historical averages, BHCs should support the chosen time periods, thresholds, and any excluded or adjusted outliers and demonstrate that loss estimates are consistent with what are expected in the stress scenario.

Legal Exposures

Since legal exposure represents a significant portion of operational losses for many BHCs, a number of BHCs have analyzed and projected legal losses separately from non-legal losses. The Federal Reserve expects BHCs to include all legal reserves and settled legal losses in their total loss estimate for operational risk. BHCs have used various methods to estimate legal losses, such as applying a judgment-based add-on for significant losses; using legal reserves; using historical averages; or creating separate regression models for the clients, products, and business practices event type. To estimate litigation losses resulting from representations and warranties liabilities related to mortgage underwriting activities, some BHCs have developed hazard-rate models based on historical loan performance to estimate default rates and then estimated repurchase claim rates.

Market Risk and Counterparty Credit Risk

BHCs that have sizeable trading operations may incur significant losses from such operations under a stress scenario due to valuation changes stemming from credit and/or market risk, which may arise as a result of moves in risk factors such as interest rates, credit spreads, or equity and commodities prices, and counterparty credit risk owing to potential deterioration in the credit quality or outright default of a trading counterparty.[37] BHCs use different techniques for estimating such potential losses. These techniques can be broadly grouped into two approaches: probabilistic approaches that generate a distribution of potential portfolio-level profit/loss (P/L) and deterministic approaches that generate a point estimate of portfolio-level losses under a specific stress scenario.

Both approaches have different strengths and weaknesses. A probabilistic approach can provide useful insight into a range of scenarios that generate stress losses in ways that a deterministic stress testing approach may not be able to do. However, the probabilistic approach is complex and often lacks transparency, and as a result, it can be difficult to communicate the relevant scenarios to senior managers and the board of directors. In addition, the challenges inherent in tying probabilistic loss estimates to specific underlying scenarios can make it difficult for management and the board of directors to readily discern what actions could be taken to mitigate portfolio losses in a given scenario. Combined, these factors complicate the use of probabilistic approaches as the primary element in an active capital planning process that reflects well-informed decisions by senior management and the board of directors. The Federal Reserve expects BHCs using a probabilistic approach to provide evidence that such an approach can generate scenarios that are potentially more severe than what was historically experienced, and also to clearly explain how BHCs use the scenarios associated with tail losses to identify and address their idiosyncratic risks.

By comparison, a deterministic approach generally produces scenarios that are easier to communicate to senior management and the board of directors. However, a deterministic approach often uses a limited set of scenarios, and may miss certain scenarios that may result in large losses. The Federal Reserve expects BHCs using a deterministic approach to demonstrate that they have considered a range of scenarios that sufficiently stress their key exposures.

For CCAR, most BHCs generally relied on a deterministic approach. BHCs using deterministic approaches often relied on statistical models—for

---

[37] Under the Federal Reserve's stress testing rules, BHCs with greater than $500 billion in total consolidated assets who are subject to the market risk rule (12 CFR part 225, appendix E) are required to apply the global market shock as part of their annual Dodd-Frank Act company-run stress tests.

example, to inform the magnitude of risk-factor movements and covariances between risk factors—and also considered multiple scenarios as part of the broader internal stress testing supporting their capital planning process. BHCs using deterministic approaches used a three-step process to generate P/L losses under a stress scenario:

1. Design and selection of stress scenarios
2. Construction and implementation of the scenario (that is, translation to risk-factor moves)
3. Revaluation (and aggregation) of position and portfolio-level P&L under the stress scenarios

The Federal Reserve expects BHCs to have robust operational and implementation practices in all areas, including position inclusion, risk-factor representations, and revaluation methods.

Stress Scenarios

Most BHCs using deterministic approaches developed a set of broad narratives and considered a number of market shock scenarios that address the breadth of the BHCs' risks before selecting the scenario included in their capital plans. In general, these BHCs used some combination of historical events and hypothetical projections to inform and develop the market shock scenarios. They also developed certain core themes or narratives for each scenario, which was sometimes supplemented with an overlay to capture additional nuances. BHCs generally developed the overlays using expert judgment based on the knowledge of their positions and market developments.

The Federal Reserve expects BHCs to consider multiple market shock scenarios as part of their internal stress testing. BHCs should develop and use stress scenarios that severely stress BHCs' mark-to-market positions and account for BHCs' idiosyncratic risks, in the event of a market-wide or firm-specific stress. In developing scenarios, BHCs should ensure that stress scenarios appropriately stress positions or products in which the BHC has a large market share (net or gross) or is a dominant player and should also consider more unusual basis risks arising from complex interlocking and interdependent positions, if such moves could result in large losses. BHCs that only use a scenario that closely mirrors the Federal Reserve's global market shock component of the severely adverse and adverse scenarios should be aware that such an approach may omit significant risks that are unique to their positions, and that such omissions could lead to a negative assessment of a firm's capital planning process. BHCs should clearly document the process they use to select stress scenarios, with sufficient justification and clear articulation of key aspects of the scenarios.[38]

Translating Scenarios to Risk Factor Shocks

Once broad scenarios were developed, BHCs translated these scenarios into concrete specification of individual risk factors that were the actual inputs to pricing models, typically using the existing risk infrastructures and processes used for risk management, such as VaR and credit valuation adjustment (CVA). Most BHCs used instantaneous market shocks for stress testing, which assumed highly stressful outcomes that have typically occurred over a period of time (days, weeks, or months) will occur instantaneously. Given the uncertainty surrounding a firm's ability to exit or manage positions during a period of severe market stress, this is an appropriate practice and suitably conservative for capital planning. Consistent with general supervisory expectations around risk-measurement processes, BHCs should clearly document the approximations and assumptions used as part of their measurement of risks under stress, assess the potential impacts, and address any deficiencies identified.[39]

The size of shocks assumed in the stress scenario is often quite large. As a result, mechanical application of such shocks to current levels of risk factors could result in implausible outcomes such as negative risk-free rates or negative forward rates. BHCs should ensure that the proposed shocks produce results that are plausible. In particular, BHCs should take care in modeling dislocations and discordant moves of risk factors that normally move similarly. Additionally, while dislocations and discordant moves are expected under stress, BHCs should have a process to assess that the resulting joint moves of risk factors are reasonable. Also, the dislocations and discordant moves implied by a stress scenario may require risk-factor mappings that deviate from the normal mappings. BHCs should clearly document instances of such deviation and provide support.[40]

---

[38] See FR Y-14A reporting form: Summary Schedule Instructions, pp. 5–6.
[39] See id., p. 6.
[40] See id., pp. 5–6.

Revaluation Methodologies and P/L Estimates

In principle, revaluation for stress testing can be carried out using the same infrastructure and calculators as conventional risk-measurement tools. However, practical revaluation methods may embed a number of approximations, which could introduce mismeasurement into the stress test results. In particular, VaR methodologies often use approximation methods for a number of reasons—for example, to economize on computational costs related to running a large number of scenarios daily. Although approximation methods may perform adequately for the risk-factor moves that are considered in normal conditions (for a small number of scenarios), BHCs should generally use "full-revaluation" methods for stress testing, given the very large risk-factor moves, especially for nonlinear positions with value dependent on multiple risk factors. BHCs can use approximation methods on a limited basis if extensive tests and analyses suggest that the potential mismeasurement from using such methods is not significant. BHCs should clearly support the process they use to ascertain the extent of such mismeasurements. Also, for certain parameters that are not easily "market-observable" and, therefore, cannot be inferred from traded instruments (e.g., correlations for credit-default baskets and correlations for certain interest-rate and exchange-rate pairs), BHCs should consider suitably perturbed values of the model parameters.

In addition, BHCs should ensure that P/L estimates under the stress scenario are relatively easy to interpret and explain. For example, BHCs with leading practices easily identified key P&L drivers in terms of positions, asset classes, and risk types. BHCs should also conduct sensitivity analysis to ensure that P/L estimates under the stress scenario are robust, without being unduly sensitive to small changes in inputs, assumptions, and modeling choices.

Counterparty and Issuer Defaults

Defaults of counterparties or issuers and/or reference entities are typically not embedded directly within the instantaneous market shock scenario. BHCs often use a model similar to that used for the incremental risk regulatory capital charge—a probabilistic approach based on some measure of PD, LGD, and EAD of counterparties or issuers—to estimate losses from possible defaults over some future horizon (e.g., to the typical margin period of risk). BHCs with leading practices also considered for their internal stress testing an explicit default scenario of one or more of their largest counterparties and/or customers. This approach has the benefit of allowing the BHC to consider targeted defaults of counterparties and customers to which the BHC has large exposures.

Risk Mitigants and Other Assumptions

Some BHCs have incorporated management responses to the stress, assuming, for example, some positions would be sold or hedged over time under the stress scenario. The Federal Reserve expects any assumptions about risk mitigation to be conservative. Where BHCs assume management actions that have the effect of reducing losses under the scenario, they should be able to demonstrate that such actions are consistent with established policy, supported by historical experience, and executable with high confidence in the market environment contemplated by the scenario. BHCs should recognize that their ability to take mitigating actions may be more limited in the stress scenario. For example, it may not be reasonable to assume that BHCs can easily sell their positions to other BHCs under the stress scenario. In addition, BHCs should avoid making unrealistic assumptions about their ability to foresee precisely how a scenario would play out, and take action on the basis of that information.

PPNR Projection Methodologies

The Capital Plan Rule requires BHCs to estimate revenue and expenses over the nine-quarter planning horizon.[41] Accordingly, BHCs should have effective processes for projecting PPNR and its revenue and expense subcomponents over the same range of stressful scenarios and environments used for estimating losses. In projecting these amounts, BHCs should consider not only their current positions, but also how their activities and business focus may evolve over time under the varying circumstances and operating environments reflected in the scenarios being used.

General Considerations for Robust PPNR Projections

As part of a comprehensive enterprise-wide scenario analysis program, BHCs should have methodologies that generate robust projections of PPNR consistent with the current and projected paths of on-and off-

---

[41] 12 CFR 225.8(d)(2)(i).

balance-sheet exposures, risk-weighted assets (RWA), and other exposure assumptions used for related loss estimation. PPNR projections should also be consistent with assumed scenario conditions and be projected in accordance with the same accounting basis that would be used to calculate relevant capital ratios. BHCs should project all key elements of PPNR at a level of granularity consistent with the materiality of revenue and expense components and sufficient to capture differing drivers of revenue and expenses across the organization. Finally, BHCs should consider the effects that regulatory changes (e.g., changes in deposit insurance coverage limits) may have on their ability to replicate historical performance or achieve stated goals.

Key assumptions that may materially affect PPNR estimates should be consistent with assumed scenario conditions and internally consistent within each scenario, particularly assumptions related to the business model and strategy (e.g., deposit growth, pricing assumptions, expense reductions, and other management actions). Management is expected to evaluate the reasonableness and timing of projected strategies, including mitigating actions taken in a stressful scenario, to ensure that the assumptions reflect realistic and achievable outcomes for a given scenario. Where possible, assumptions should be supported by quantitative analysis or empirical evidence.

In all cases, BHCs should ensure that projections (including those of PPNR, loss, balance sheet size and composition, and RWA) present a coherent story within each scenario. BHCs should clearly establish a relationship among revenue, expenses, the balance sheet, and any applicable off-balance-sheet items and document how their process generates a consistent and coherent evolution of these items over the course of the scenario.[42] For example, origination assumptions should be the same for projecting loan balances, related loan fees, origination costs, and loan losses. Similarly, there should be coherence among trading revenue projections, trading assets, trading liabilities, and trading RWA projections. Management should document the relationships among these items and avoid cases where outcomes move in counterintuitive directions.[43]

Observed PPNR Projection Practices

The translation of macroeconomic assumptions into projections of PPNR over a range of stressful scenarios and environments can take many forms, and BHCs used a variety of approaches and models to make these projections. BHCs with stronger practices demonstrated strong interactions among central planning functions, business lines, and the treasury group, with an open flow of information and a robust challenge process. At these BHCs, the role of the central group was not just to aggregate components of PPNR projections. In some cases, the corporate planning areas also provided independent projections that were compared to the aggregated business line results as a part of the challenge process. At other BHCs, the corporate planning group derived the PPNR projections, which were then discussed and challenged by business lines. Both approaches resulted in better-supported assumptions and projections than approaches in which the central group simply aggregated projections made by others.

In addition, BHCs with stronger practices made projections based on a full exploration of the most relevant relationships between assumed scenario conditions and revenues and expenses. At these BHCs, business-line expertise was leveraged in the development of methodologies. A key part of this exploration was determining the way that revenues and expenses were segmented for projection purposes. BHCs with stronger practices did not rely exclusively on the line-item definitions in regulatory reports, though these BHCs often established a process to clearly map internal BHC reporting conventions to the various line items on the FR Y-14 schedules.

In contrast, BHCs with lagging practices lacked clear processes for translating assumed scenario conditions into revenue and expense projections. Frequently, it was observed that one or more material components of their projections appeared inconsistent with scenario conditions. In some cases, projections of certain revenue and expense components relied heavily on management judgment, which was not transparent, well supported, or subject to a robust challenge process. In other cases, revenue estimates varied from historical experience and conventional expectations, and management provided no documented support or analysis around the reasonableness and sensitivity of modeling assumptions. Overall, data limitations, unclear or unsubstantiated management assumptions, and poor documentation were the problems most prevalent across the BHCs.

---

[42] See 12 CFR 225.8(d)(i)–(ii); FR Y-14A reporting form: Summary Schedule Instructions, pp. 5–6.

[43] See id.

Another commonly observed practice for estimating PPNR under stressed conditions was the adjustment of budget or baseline estimates, with budget estimates largely qualitatively derived through input from a variety of business lines and/or stakeholders across the BHC. Although a process of adjusting baseline estimates is not problematic in itself, some BHCs relied heavily on baseline estimates to develop stress scenario outcomes without considering favorable strategic actions and assumptions incorporated into baseline results that might not be realistic or feasible under stressed conditions. If a BHC derives stressed estimates by applying a stress overlay to baseline estimates, it should demonstrate the link between baseline estimates and baseline conditions, demonstrate the appropriateness of the overlay based on the differing conditions between the scenarios, and appropriately consider changes in management actions or other related assumptions under a stress scenario.

BHCs with weaker practices used models with low predictive power, in part due to data limitations. BHCs should not use weak models just for the sake of using a modeled approach to PPNR. Some BHCs used weak models either as a frame of reference or a starting point to translate economic factors into estimates of key PPNR components, but then adjusted the results using expert judgment. In such cases, BHCs should thoroughly explain and document why results, once adjusted, are consistent with the scenario conditions.[44] In cases where models have low predictive power, BHCs with stronger practices found other ways to compensate, such as using industry-level models with BHC-specific market share assumptions to project revenue. In all cases, BHCs with stronger practices provided supplemental analysis describing why the approach was appropriate.

In cases where BHC-specific data were limited, BHCs with stronger practices used external data to augment and extend their internal data. BHCs with weaker practices relied on models that were overly influenced by limited data covering a single economic cycle. This approach is particularly problematic if the BHC also experienced favorable conditions, such as a significant recovery, during the single cycle, which might not recur in future downturns. In some cases, data were limited to as few as 10 quarters, which would not encompass a period of economic weakening or be sufficient to estimate a robust model, and thus would not be appropriate for considering potential results in a downturn. Many BHCs cited challenges due to systems mergers or changes that limited data availability, but failed to adequately compensate for these limitations by supplementing internal data with external industry data, where appropriate, or by considering whether longer time series of available aggregate data would be preferable to a shorter time series of more granular data.

Some BHCs with weaker practices made business model and strategy assumptions (e.g., new business, expense reductions, the assumption of mitigating actions) that were not consistent with stressed scenario conditions and the intent of a capital planning and stress testing exercise. For example, management assumed it would be able to drastically reduce loan origination activity, cut expenses, or take other mitigating actions in a severely adverse scenario without considering the longer-term consequences on the BHC's strategy and operating structure.

The following sections provide specific expectations for projecting key components of PPNR, as well as summary points on observed range of practice.

Net Interest Income

Net interest income projections are closely linked to many other elements of a BHC's capital plan. Balance sheet assumptions used to project net interest income should be consistent with balance sheet assumptions considered as part of loss estimation as well as with other asset and liability management assumptions. Loan pricing should be consistent with both scenario conditions and competitive and strategic factors, including projected changes to the size of the portfolio. Deposit projections should incorporate the impact of strategic plans and pricing on deposit growth or decline, in addition to scenario factors.

Net interest income projections are expected to incorporate the balances and contractual terms of current portfolio holdings as well as the behavioral characteristics of these portfolios. The methods BHCs use to project their net interest income should be able to capture dynamic conditions for both current and projected balance sheet positions. Such conditions include but are not limited to prepayment rates, new business spreads, re-pricing rates due to changes in yield curves, behavior of embedded optionality such

---

[44] See id.

as caps or floors, call options, and/or changes in loan performance (that is, transition to nonperforming or default status) consistent with loss estimates.

Some BHCs specified product characteristics and conducted analysis around these characteristics (e.g., repricing behavior, line utilizations) both for current assets and new originations in order to understand the variance in behaviors under the different scenarios considered. They also attempted to capture the product mix changes that would occur as a result of customer and market conditions (e.g., changes in domestic deposit mix due to anticipated growth in demand for time deposits for a specified scenario). BHCs with stronger documentation practices provided detailed tables explaining underlying assumptions such as balance drivers and spread and growth assumptions by product.

Some BHCs partially integrated loss projections into net interest income projections but did not adequately align all projection-related assumptions. For example, these BHCs might take the full loan loss projections and allocate them across the portfolios based on the current mix of nonperformance across those loan portfolios, without considering the changing relative performance of those portfolios over the course of the scenario. Other BHCs were unable to demonstrate coherence between net interest income projections and loss projections, generally because one or both modeling approaches did not fully capture the behavioral characteristics of the loan portfolio.

BHCs with stronger practices had net interest income projection methodologies that captured adjustments in the amortization of discounts or premiums for assets held at a value other than par that would occur under various scenarios. Under FASB Statement No. 91,[45] yields would adjust under varying scenarios as amortization schedules change due to changes in expected payment speeds.

For pricing, many BHCs assumed a constant spread to a designated index. BHCs with stronger practices considered whether this assumption was consistent with historical experience and assumed scenario conditions as well as the BHC's strategy as reflected in the balance sheet projections. Some BHCs recognized that new business pricing could differ as a result of tightening or widening of spreads and documented these assumptions.

Non-Interest Income

BHCs are expected to produce stressed projections of non-interest income that are consistent with assumed scenario conditions, as well as with stated business strategies. Due to inherent challenges in estimating certain non-interest income components, some BHCs used more than one method and/or employed benchmark analysis to inform estimates. Stronger methodologies estimated non-interest income at a granular-enough level to capture key risk factors or characteristics specific to an activity or product. For example, for asset management, many BHCs used different methods to project revenue from brokerage activities and fund management activities.

Like all aspects of PPNR, internal consistency between non-interest income and other assumptions such as projected paths for the balance sheet and RWA is important. BHCs should establish relationships between material components of non-interest income and the balance sheet for components that are highly correlated with the path of the balance sheet, such as some kinds of loan-related fee income. BHCs with trading assets should document how trading revenue projections are linked to trading assets, trading liabilities, and trading RWA and how all these elements are consistent with conditions in the stress scenario.[46] BHCs with business profiles driven by off-balance-sheet items should document how revenue projections are linked to on- and off-balance-sheet behavior.[47] Although relationships between revenue and trading assets or off-balance-sheet items may be weak over short periods, BHCs should nevertheless establish a procedure for projecting relevant balance sheet and RWA categories in support of those revenues and test for the reasonableness of the implied return on assets (ROA). If a BHC estimates trading or private equity revenue by tying balance changes to changes in broad indices, the BHC should establish the level of sensitivity of its positions relative to the indices and not automatically assume a perfect correlation between the two.

---

[45] Financial Accounting Standards Board, "Accounting for Nonrefundable Fees and Costs Associated with Originating or Acquiring Loans and Initial Direct Costs of Leases—an Amendment of FASB Statements No. 13, 60, and 65 and a Rescission of FASB Statement No. 17 (Issued 12/86)," FASB Statement No. 91.

[46] See FR Y-14A reporting form: Summary Schedule Instructions, p. 5.

[47] 12 CFR 225.8(d)(3)(iii); see also FR Y-14A reporting form: Summary Schedule Instructions, pp. 5–6.

BHCs with mortgage servicing right (MSR) assets should ensure that delinquency, default, and voluntary prepayment assumptions are robust and scenario-dependent. These models should capture macroeconomic variables, especially home prices. For those BHCs that routinely hedge MSR exposure, hedge assumptions and results for enterprise-wide scenario analysis should reflect the stress scenario. Some BHCs assumed a perfect or near-perfect hedge relationship between changes in the value of their MSR and hedge portfolio, and captured the ineffectiveness of the hedge under the stress scenario through the net carry, transaction costs, and/or bid-ask spread components. BHCs with stronger practices used an optimization routine that dynamically rebalanced the hedge portfolio each quarter.

BHCs with stronger practices considered individual business models and client profiles when projecting revenue and fee income from various business activities. BHCs with stronger practices also considered capacity constraints when estimating mortgage loan production and loan sales over the scenario horizon, whereas BHCs with weaker practices assumed significant increases in volume without regard to market saturation or other factors. Other weaker practices observed included using the same strategic business assumptions in both the baseline and stress scenarios and making favorable assumptions around new business and/or market share gains. For example, some BHCs assumed that all baseline initiatives would be implemented in stress scenarios without interruption or changes to the outcomes.

In addition, BHCs with weaker practices did not show sufficiently stressed declines in revenue relative to assumed scenario conditions, despite stated correlations to macroeconomic and other drivers. For example, while many BHCs showed significant declines in credit card gross-interchange fee revenue due to declines in consumer spending, some BHCs also assumed that significant declines in marketing expenses recorded as contra-revenue would more than offset the declines in gross interchange revenue, resulting in an increase in net revenue. Other BHCs assumed revenue components, such as fees or trading revenue, could not fall below historical levels.

Further, BHCs with weaker practices considered only a very limited set of scenario variables and/or drivers in establishing relationships, which resulted in estimates that appeared inconsistent with the scenario. For example, some BHCs used interest rates only to project origination activity or solely used asset balances (instead of the number of accounts) to estimate account fees. Other BHCs simply regressed high-level revenue items against scenario factors rather than considering how scenario conditions would affect the key drivers of those line items (such as volume). For instance, modeling interchange revenues or asset management fees is likely to be less effective than modeling customer spending or assets under management, respectively, given the scenario being used, and then considering fee and/or rate movement.

Non-Interest Expense

BHCs should fully consider the various impacts of the assumed scenario conditions on their non-interest expense projections, including costs that are likely to increase during a downturn. For example, items such as other real estate owned or credit-collection costs may spike, whereas management may have some ability to control other expenses. Like other projections, non-interest expense projections should be consistent with balance sheet and revenue estimates and should reflect the same strategic business assumptions. BHCs with weaker practices did not account for additional headcount needs in certain areas, nor for any corresponding changes to compensation expense associated with increased collections activity resulting from declines in portfolio quality and/or increased underwriting activity to support any assumed portfolio growth.

To the extent the projections assume mitigating actions to offset revenue declines, BHCs should demonstrate that such actions are attainable in the scenario, given assumed asset levels and the resources necessary to support operations. If the projections embed material expense reductions, such assumptions should be supported with analysis of historical data or empirical evidence and subject to challenge and review. BHCs with weaker practices assumed mitigating actions consistent with past actions but failed to consider how differences in the business environment and the severity of the economic conditions might affect their ability to execute such actions. BHCs are expected to evaluate the timing of projected strategies and their impact on future revenue, expenses, and operating structure.

BHCs with stronger practices had estimation methodologies that considered the drivers of individual expense items and the sensitivity of those drivers to changing scenario conditions and business strategies. They considered the timing of non-interest expense cuts and recognized that the BHC might not be able to react to a developing stressful scenario immediately or might be subject to existing contractual obligations that could not be altered. BHCs with weaker practices generated non-interest expense estimates that appeared unrealistic in light of assumed scenario conditions. Some BHCs assumed that they could immediately reduce costs through dramatic cuts in marketing and rewards programs, compensation, or other discretionary expenses. Projecting sizeable reductions in key expense components without providing sufficient support as to the reasonableness of the cuts, how management intends to realize the cuts, and how the cuts will affect future revenue is not acceptable. Additionally, such assumptions imply perfect knowledge of the conditions as they unfold, rather than a series of independent decisions that would be made by management as the scenario unfolds.

Assessing Capital Adequacy Impact

Balance Sheet and RWAs

BHCs should have a well-documented process for generating projections of the size and composition of on- and off-balance sheet positions and RWA over the scenario horizon.[48] Balance projections are a key input to enterprise-wide scenario analysis given their direct impact on the estimation of losses, PPNR, and RWA. Estimating the evolution of balance sheet size and composition under stress integrates many interrelated features. For example, loan balances and the stock of AFS securities at a point in time will depend upon origination, purchase, and sale activity from period to period, as well as maturities, prepayments, and defaults. Due to complexities related to dynamically projecting and integrating various components (e.g., originations, prepayments and defaults), most BHCs made direct projections of balances for each major segment of the balance sheet (e.g., loans, deposits, trading assets and liabilities, and other assets) for each quarter of the scenario horizon.

BHCs often faced challenges in integrating the ultimate balance projections with other aspects—for example, borrower or depositor behavior. BHCs with stronger practices separately considered the drivers of change to asset and funding balances, such as contractual paydowns, modeled prepayments, nonperformance, and new business activity for assets, rather than simply projecting targeted balances directly. At these BHCs, each element was separately assessed for consistency with scenario conditions and other management assumptions. BHCs with stronger practices also either directly considered the impact of these various factors in their balance projections or had procedures to evaluate the reasonableness of any implied behavior by including input from business-line leaders in the process and iterating to reasonable estimates in a well-supported and transparent manner.

BHCs should clearly establish and incorporate into their scenario analysis the relationships among and between revenue, expense, and on- and off-balance-sheet items under stressful conditions. Most BHCs used asset-liability management (ALM) software as a part of their enterprise-wide scenario-analysis toolkit, which helps integrate these items. BHCs that do not use ALM software must have a process that integrates balance sheet projections with revenue, loss, and new business projections. BHCs with more tightly integrated procedures were better able to ensure appropriate relationships among the scenario conditions, losses, expenses, revenue, and balances.

As noted above, BHCs should not rely on favorable assumptions that cannot be reasonably assured in stress scenarios given the high level of uncertainty around market conditions. Examples of aggressive or favorable balance sheet assumptions include (1) large changes in asset mix that serve to decrease BHCs' risk weights and improve post-stress capital ratios but that are not adequately supported or reflected in PPNR or loss estimates; (2) "flight-to-quality" assumptions and funding mix changes that increase deposits and reduce the dollar cost of funding; (3) significant balance sheet shrinkage with no consideration of the potential losses associated with reducing positions in periods of market stress; and (4) operating margin improvement. BHCs that make favorable assumptions should have sufficient evidence that they can be reasonably assured in the assumed stress scenario.

BHCs' RWA projections should be based on corresponding projections of on- and off-balance-sheet exposures and their risk attributes and should be consistent with the severity of the stress conditions under each scenario. For general credit-risk exposures, BHCs should project balances for material asset categories with sufficient granularity to facilitate application of regulatory risk-weighting approaches associated with different asset categories. For trading exposures, BHCs should translate changes in scenario variables into risk-parameter

---

[48] 12 CFR 225.8(d)(2)(i)(A); see also FR Y-14A reporting form: Summary Schedule Instructions, p. 6.

estimates that drive RWA calculations (e.g., the potential for RWA per dollar of some trading book positions to increase in periods of higher levels of general market volatility). Where RWA projections are based on internal risk models, BHCs should not assume any RWA reductions from potential data or model enhancements to RWA calculation methodologies over the projection period. In all cases, BHCs should document any assumptions made as part of the balance sheet and RWA projection process and perform independent reviews and validations of balance sheet and RWA projection methodologies and resulting estimates.[49]

Allowance for Loan and Lease Losses (ALLL)

BHCs should maintain an adequate ALLL along the scenario path and at the end of the scenario horizon. Reserve adequacy should be assessed against projected size, composition, and risk characteristics of the loan portfolio throughout the scenario horizon. In general, the ALLL build and release should be consistent with the scenario path, portfolio credit quality, loss recognition approach, loan loss estimates, and loan portfolio balance projections (including any portfolio growth assumptions). If BHCs use estimation approaches that implicitly delay the recognition of losses, such as net charge-off models, they should adequately build reserves to account for losses not recognized during the scenario horizon. If the approach relies on top-down coverage levels, BHCs should compare coverage ratios and loss-emergence periods to historical stress environments and to internal policies and explain the differences if material differences exist.

Aggregation of Projections

BHCs should have a well-established and consistently executed process for aggregating loss, revenue and expense, and on- and off-balance sheet and RWA estimates, as part of enterprise-wide scenario analysis, to assess the post-stress impact of those estimates on capital ratios. BHCs that are more effective at implementing such a process have established centralized groups with responsibility for

- combining loss, revenue, balance sheet, and RWA projections;

- providing strong governance and controls around the process;
- ensuring coherence of component estimates and aggregate results; and
- applying and documenting any adjustments.[50]

These centralized groups have been able to source estimates from a range of internal parties involved in enterprise-wide scenario analysis and develop consolidated pro forma financial results that are internally consistent and conform to accounting standards.

BHCs should develop a governance structure around the enterprise-wide scenario analysis process that provides for a robust analysis and challenge of the coherence of the aggregate results and determine whether any adjustments need to be made based on the analysis. In particular, BHCs should assess whether the paths of individual loss and revenue components are consistent with the paths of balance sheet and RWA estimates and the overall scenario path. For example, an increase in PPNR amid declining balances would appear generally inconsistent and should warrant further investigation. In assessing consolidated financial results, BHCs should account for any potential changes in relationships between losses and financial performance drivers during periods of stress.

BHCs should have good understanding of instances when exposures with similar underlying risk characteristics that are part of different portfolios or business lines exhibit different sensitivities to scenario conditions. BHCs should identify instances where the differences are due to inconsistent assumptions or modeling approaches that require management attention, rather than differences in accounting treatment. In addition, if a BHC's enterprise-wide scenario analysis results in post-stress outcomes that are more favorable than those under baseline conditions, BHCs should critically evaluate the reasonableness and consistency of assumptions across portfolios, business lines, and other areas of loss and revenue estimation.

BHCs that had an effective aggregation process leveraged their business planning and financial and regulatory reporting systems as part of that process. Using standalone tools or spreadsheets in the aggregation process is a weak process. If a BHC needs to

---

[49] See id.

[50] See id.

use standalone tools or spreadsheets due to systems limitation, management should ensure robust controls are in place, including access and change controls, and should maintain an audit trail and document all approvals for any adjustments made. BHCs should also have reconciliation procedures and data-quality and logic checks in place to ensure that the results from the enterprise-wide scenario analysis reconcile to both management reporting and regulatory reports, with a transparent mapping between various reporting taxonomies.

BHCs with weaker practices had limited or no reconciliation procedures or other controls in place to ensure the integrity, completeness, and accuracy of the consolidated post-stress capital metrics. BHCs with weaker practices also had no process to ensure consistency in the BHC-wide application of scenario assumptions and management adjustments, and had weak governance and documentation standards.

Concluding Observations

The goal of this publication is to outline the Federal Reserve's expectations for internal capital planning at large BHCs and to highlight the range of current practice as observed during the 2013 CCAR. This discussion is intended to provide a more comprehensive set of criteria to assist BHC management in assessing their current capital planning processes and in designing and implementing improvements to those processes, as well as to provide insight to a broader audience about the key aspects of BHCs' capital planning practices.

Internal capital planning practices have evolved considerably since the financial crisis and the implementation of the Federal Reserve's Capital Plan Rule in 2011. BHCs have made advances in the identification and measurement of the risks to their capital and in the integration of stress testing and capital planning into their broader strategic planning processes. The fundamental insight governing the Federal Reserve's expectations about capital planning is the importance of having a forward-looking perspective on the risks to a BHC's capital resources under severely stressful conditions. In particular, a forward-looking perspective involves understanding how a BHC's revenue-generating capacity and potential losses could be affected in stressed economic and financial market conditions; understanding the particular vulnerabilities arising from its business model and activities; and having a capital policy in place that governs the BHC's capital actions under both "normal" and stressed economic conditions. These elements represent substantial conceptual and operational improvements in capital planning that go well beyond simple consideration of current and expected future capital ratios.

While many of the large BHCs subject to the Capital Plan Rule have made substantial improvements in capital planning, there is still considerable room for advancement across a number of dimensions. Areas where some BHCs continue to fall short of leading practice include

- not being able to show how all their risks were accounted for in their capital planning processes;
- using stress scenarios and modeling techniques that did not address the particular vulnerabilities of the BHC's business model and activities;
- generating projections for at least some components of loss, revenue, or expenses using approaches that were not robust, transparent, and/or repeatable, or that did not fully capture the impact of stressed conditions;
- having capital policies that did not clearly articulate a BHC's capital goals and targets, did not provide analytical support for how these goals and targets were determined to be appropriate, and/or were not comprehensive or detailed enough to provide clear guidance about how the BHC would respond as its capital position changed in different economic circumstances; and
- having less-than-robust governance or controls around the capital planning process, including around fundamental risk-identification, -measurement, and -management practices that are among the critical elements that support robust capital planning.

All the BHCs that participated in CCAR faced challenges across one or more of these areas. And although many BHCs demonstrated leading practices in several dimensions of capital planning, the leading capital planning practices identified in this paper will continue to evolve as new data become available, economic conditions change, new products and businesses introduce new risks, and estimation techniques advance further. As the frontier of capital planning practice advances, the Federal Reserve's expectations for how BHCs implement the requirements of the Capital Plan Rule and the related company-run stress testing required under the Dodd-Frank Act will also evolve.[51] Such advances in capital planning practices will enhance the health and stability of individual BHCs and of the overall banking system.

---

[51] 12 CFR part 252, subpart G.

www.ingramcontent.com/pod-product-compliance
Lightning Source LLC
Chambersburg PA
CBHW081801170526
45167CB00008B/3280